# SAVING LILLIAN BAY

## MIRACLES HAPPEN

By Ron Knight

As Told By Brad Beatty
With Lillian Bay Beatty

Cover Design and Book Layout by Brand Eleven Eleven

For information regarding permission,
Contact us at our website
www.upauthors.com or www.brand1111.com
Write to:
Brand Eleven Eleven
3516 N. Lockwood Ridge Road
Sarasota, FL 34234

Printed in the U.S.A.

Printed November 2012

This book is dedicated to Lillian Bay,
along with the many that saved her life.

# FORWARD

The community on the island of Boca Grande is a special, small community that will pull together and support one another in a time of need. This became evident when, Brad Beatty, the outgoing and friendly UPS driver faced a devastating situation as his baby girl fought for her life.

It was unquestionable, when hearing about Lillian Bay's condition and the overwhelming hardship on her family, that I would tap into all the resources in the community to help. Boca Grande responded quickly to provide Lillian Bay and her family support during a most difficult time. It's been incredibly inspiring to see people come forward with generosity and kindness.

The future holds great promise for Lillian Bay and we will all continue to follow her progress with hope of continued success.

*Rusty Hager, Chairman of the Board at Hager Companies*

♥

Carol and I care about the well-being of Brad and Lilly. We've assisted with Lilly's medical needs, shared encouraging words with Brad, and have always tried to be there for them whenever an emergency arose. We enjoy spending time with Brad and Lilly, in so many ways, even if it's just to have a relaxing afternoon together. It is wonderful to see the community of Boca Grande come together to support Brad and Lilly. I hope that this book impacts their lives for the better, along with everyone who enjoys and shares their story.

*John Walter of Boca Grande*

# SAVING LILLIAN BAY

## MIRACLES HAPPEN

By Ron Knight

As Told By Brad Beatty
With Lillian Bay Beatty

*"Life is God's novel. Let him write it."*

**~ Isaac Bashevis Singer**

# Moments of Destiny

*"The greatest in the Kingdom of Heaven is the one who humbles himself and becomes like this child."*

**~ Matthew 18:4**

Millions of dollars, endless prayers, and several miracles were needed to save her life. She did not understand medical reports, or the odds of living. She has not been on this earth long enough to grasp the idea of fighting with all her strength.

No one would expect a newborn child to understand the whisper in her ear, as her father tells his daughter, "I love you. And I will do everything I can to save you."

Fate placed her father in a position to raise the millions needed for medical expenses. It was nothing short of God-like, as the right people were in the right place, at the right time. A community came together, refusing to give up. Even the circumstances that led to this book went beyond a fluke, chance, or coincidence. Like everything that occurred to this point, it was spiritual.

God will show us a community of family and friends that pulled their resources together with unselfish love to save a child's life. We will be shown a father that refused to let his daughter be taken from this world.

Most importantly, we will be shown a little girl that does not comprehend wisdom, love, or faith, and yet, displays those gifts with each breath.

Today, and everyday, let us humble ourselves . . . and be like this child.

This is the story of Lillian Bay . . .

♥

Brad Beatty has been a UPS driver for twelve years, stationed in Port Charlotte, Florida. UPS drivers bid on routes and are placed in areas based on seniority. George Fox had been with UPS for thirty years when he decided it was time to retire. The route that he would be leaving was Boca Grande.

On dare of all things, Brad decided to bid on the route. Unbeknownst to Brad, this decision would completely change every aspect of his life.

Boca Grande is a small residential community on Gasparilla Island in Southwest Florida, known for its downtown, which many describe as both charming and historic. The island is famous for its sugar sand beaches, blue ocean water, and world-class fishing.

The average home sells for around $1.2 million, with residents that consist of politicians, CEO's of Fortune 500 companies, and some of the wealthiest people in the world. The residents are also some of the kindest people in the world.

There are no gas stations on Boca Grande, so most of the residents use golf carts as their main form of transportation. Everyone knows each other on the island, which creates a tight nit community.

As for Brad, he certainly had a considerable challenge ahead, since the previous UPS driver, had spent years building relationships with all the prominent residents on Boca Grande. For any new driver, this route can be extremely difficult to master.

On Brad's first day, with no map and plenty of confidence, he discovered how complicated Boca Grande really was. The residents expected packages to be delivered in a certain place. There were mazes of endless streets. And the touristy downtown traffic made it nearly impossible for Brad to succeed. He spent most of his time on the phone, asking for help and directions.

Over the next month Brad got a handle on things. He also realized how polite and caring the residents of Boca Grande really were. In fact, he did not consider anyone a "customer," but instead, he considered every resident and business owner his friend.

One day on his route, Brad saw a beautiful woman on a balcony of the local newspaper building, the Boca Beacon. She giggled and smiled while talking on the phone, pacing back and forth in her gorgeous summer dress. Brad did not want to be caught staring, but he could not help himself. This was the fairytale, "Love at first sight."

Two days later, a fishing guide on Boca Grande named Sandy Melvin informed Brad, "I have the perfect girl I want you to meet." Brad hesitated. His father had died a year ago of pancreatic cancer and Brad was still trying to get over the emotions of his father being gone. Brad did not want his date thinking that he was too sad or depressing.

After considering it for a few moments, he decided to give it a shot.

"Her name is Nikki," Sandy explained. "She works for me during tarpon season on one of my boats and she works at the Boca Beacon."

Brad could not believe it. The Boca Beacon! What were the chances that he was being setup with the same woman he fell in love with from a distance?

Brad turned to Sandy, formed a grin, then said, "Do you want to see me make a fool out of myself?"

Before Sandy could respond to that odd question, Brad took off, ran up the stairs of the Boca Beacon building, burst into the room, looked at Nikki and said, "Ddddd…do you like fishing? Maybe we could meet up sometime?"

Ugg . . .

It wasn't the smoothest date request, but it worked. They exchanged phone numbers.

Over the next few months, Brad and Nikki did not spend one day apart. In fact, they vowed that they would never go a day without seeing each other. "Don't break the streak," they would say.

When they married on March 7th, 2009, it was a perfect spring day on Gasparilla Island. However, Nikki had not been feeling well at the wedding reception. A week later, she discovered why…

She was pregnant.

♥

## A Spiritual Message from Lillian Bay.

*God had a plan for me, long before anyone knew that I would arrive. And you can trust that God had a plan for you, long before you were born. He is in control of your life. Trust Him and believe in His plan for you.*

# Rare Condition

*"Behold, children are a heritage from the Lord."*

**~ Psalm 127:3**

A pleasant wave of joy swept over them when the doctor said, "You are going to have a girl!"

Brad and Nikki brought out the best in each other. Nothing could get in their way of being happy. Their life was not perfect, but when you are that much in love, your inner world becomes flawless.

They were living together in Nikki's house, while still making payments on Brad's home. With Brad at UPS and Nikki still at the Boca Beacon, their income was just enough to manage the extra bills. In fact, everything in their life was manageable.

However, no one in the world could have prepared them for what was about to happen.

♥

Twenty-one weeks into the pregnancy, Nikki had her first ultrasound. Their daughter was absolutely beautiful. It was a perfect moment. The baby was in good health and on schedule.

At thirty-two weeks pregnant when she went in for another ultrasound appointment, Dr. Gregush, her obstetrician, told them, "There appears to be a black spot on your baby's neck." The next statement was even more crushing. "I'm sorry, but I don't know what it is."

Dr. Gregush referred Brad and Nikki to a specialist at Maternal Fetal Medicine in Port Charlotte, Florida. A full examine was conducted on September 17th, 2009. They were told, "Your baby has a mass on her lower jaw." They went on to explain that the problem was unfamiliar to the technicians and doctors.

Of course, Brad and Nikki were unable to grasp what the doctor was saying.

How was this possible?

The child was healthy just eleven weeks ago. Now there is something wrong?

Maybe it's something that can be treated.

It was then, Brad and Nikki's difficult journey would really begin.

♥

Brad told his mother the bad news. She made a call to her good friend, Pat Starr, and explained the situation. Ten years ago, Pat had formally worked as a secretary for Dr. Washington Hill in Sarasota, Florida. Pat's husband suggested that she call Dr. Hill and see if he would give a more comprehensive examination and opinion.

"I left a message and explained the condition of the baby, along with the circumstances," Pat said to Brad's mother. "Just keep in mind that it's been ten years since I worked for him. He might not call me back."

The doctor indeed returned Pat's phone call and requested that Brad and Nikki come in that following Monday. Unfortunately, Dr.

Hill could not provide any more information because of the rarity of the condition. He then referred Brad and Nikki to All Children's Hospital in St. Petersburg, Florida.

Dr. Hill finished by saying, "You are going to need a lot of prayers. Her chances are not good."

♥

The diagnosis was Cystic Hygroma on her throat, along with Hygroma on her tongue. It is a very rare condition that many doctors have not encountered, even at All Children's Hospital.

*Rare condition.*

*Treatments unknown.*

*A disease on your child's throat and tongue.*

Doctors did their best to explain the problems with the fetus, the odds of the fetus surviving, and what will transpire with the fetus in the weeks ahead. Brad and Nikki cringed, hating that the doctors continued to discuss their baby as if she was a medical glitch, or an anomaly.

This was a child. A human. Their baby girl.

Tears drained from Brad and Nikki's eyes. Strength seeped from their bodies. Words from the doctors that had been spoken over the past month replayed in their minds.

"There is a black spot on your baby's neck."

"I'm sorry, but I don't know what this is. You need to see a specialist."

"A mass is on your baby's lower jaw."

"We are unfamiliar with this kind of problem."

"Rare condition."

"Cystic Hygroma, something that most doctors have never encountered."

"Her chances are not good."

"You are going to need lots of prayers."

Brad lowered his head, with tears drizzling from his swollen eyes. He blocked out the words from others, folded his hands, squeezing so hard that his knuckles turned white. He could hardly breathe. Hardly think.

Why should he simply accept that his child was going to die? He couldn't accept that she was not meant to live in this world. Why couldn't his baby have at least a chance to live?

The noise in the hospital disappeared. Sounds faded to nothing. Brad longed for silence. He needed a few seconds of peace, without the doctors voices. He did not want to hear any more words like odds, probability, or likelihood.

Brad wanted to be alone with God. At this moment, God was the only voice that mattered.

♥

## A Spiritual Message from Lillian Bay.

*Even in the womb of my mother, I can hear the voices around me. I cannot understand the words, but I can sense the fear. It is hard to be alone, because the world seems so noisy.*

*I've already learned that God likes to whisper, so I have to listen extra hard to hear His voice. That is what I am doing right now…hearing His voice.*

# FINDING THE WAY

*"...He will never fail you."*

**~ 1 Peter 4:19**

Countless trips were made to All Children's Hospital and doctors offices. Preparations had to be made, because no one really knew what to expect. A team of doctors would have to be ready at the time of delivery.

Unforeseen problems seemed likely.

Dr. Karen A. Raimer would deliver the baby. Also needed was Dr. Thomas Andrews, an Ear, Nose and Throat Specialist, along with a Pediatric Otolaryngologist, an Anesthesiologist and many assistants for pain management.

If the child survived the birth, many other doctors would be needed.

## Lillian Bay, Medical Report

Date: TBD

Notes:

- Surgery done by Dr. Karen A. Raimer.
- Follow-up with Dr. Thomas Andrews, the Pediatric Ear Nose and Throat Specialist.
- Speech therapy, along with swallowing and eating treatments.
- Physical and developmental therapy.
- Checkups with Dr. Susan Williams, Pediatrician.

Lillian Bay Beatty

*If the child survived the birth.*

Those words could not have been more terrifying. Regardless, doctors continued their plans. Later, if the baby were born, more trips to All Children's Hospital, Bayfront Medical Center, St. Petersburg Maternal, the Pediatric Pulmonary Association, and appointments with laboratory physicians would be needed.

The list went on and on. Their future medical bills would be enormous.

How would they manage raising a child with such needs, while they both had jobs? How were they going to make the countless trips to doctor's appointments?

Even with a substantial team of medical providers and specialists, Brad and Nikki were still told that they should prepare for the worst. Brad and Nikki's money already began to drain with each passing day, while the doctors warning continued to haunt their thoughts.

*If the child survived the birth.*

♥

Their stress levels stretched beyond what a young couple should have to endure. The world around them continued to move, but they were trapped in a motionless state of worry.

Neither Brad nor Nikki could hear anything spiritual, or uplifting, because it did not seem those words existed. God was speaking to them, but only in a whisper.

Lean on Me.

Trust Me.

Be confident in the Lord.

Do not rely on your own understanding.

Think with your heart, not your mind.

Worrying is a lack of trust in God.

Then, something changed in Brad and Nikki. Why should they have to prepare for the worst? Everyone else was already doing that. Brad and Nikki wanted to believe that somehow they were going to be parents. Their child would be born. Their little girl would survive and live a long, happy life. Their thinking began to change.

When the child survives the birth, many plans will be needed.

We will figure out a way to cover the bills.

We will find a way to make the trips to the hospital and doctor appointments.

They decided to be ready for their daughter's arrival. Nikki traded in her small car for a larger family vehicle. They decorated the baby's room. And most importantly, they decided to give their little girl a name.

Her first name would be after an aunt on Nikki's side of the family. Her middle name would be after a place where Brad's brother Todd had lived, called Magens Bay on Saint Thomas; a place that has the most beautiful beaches in the world.

Brad and Nikki decided not to tell anyone their little girl's name. At least, not until she was born.

♥

## A Spiritual Message from Lillian Bay.

*God saw me as a child. My parents saw me as a child. Because of their faith, I became a child.*

*I hope that you can picture great days ahead. If you cannot, then sit down and draw a picture of great things. That is what I will be doing very soon!*

# 11/11/09

*"What is faith? It is the confident assurance that what we hope for is going to happen. It is the evidence of things we cannot see."*

**~ Hebrews 11:1**

Nikki was wheeled into a small room with Brad next to her. Also at the hospital was Brad's mother Marsha, Brad's cousin Lori, Brad's best friend Larry "Heavy Duty" Frazer, Nikki's mother Vickie, and several other friends and relatives of the family.

Entering the room was Dr. Karen A. Raimer. She asked, "What is going to be your baby's name?"

This would be the first time that Brad and Nikki revealed their daughter's name to everyone. "Lillian Bay Beatty."

Moments later, Nikki was taken to the delivery room.

♥

Because of the mass on Lillian's neck, a team of specialists would have to do an exit procedure in order to give Lillian a chance. The baby would remain on the umbilical cord, while Nikki's belly was open, so that doctors can examine the airway for the baby.

Suddenly, the cord ruptured. Nikki had lost over six hundred cc's of blood. The doctors had to create an airway in order give Lillian a chance to breathe. Everyone had been prepared for the worst-case scenarios. This was certainly classified as worst-case.

A mother's instinct took over. Nikki came out of the anesthesia. Through fogged eyes, she saw her stomach sliced open. Her child was still on the umbilical cord. Blood seemed to be everywhere, as the doctors continued with the procedure. They were doing everything possible to save Lillian.

The doctors were trying to save Nikki as well.

♥

Nikki peeled her eyes open. She was in a small room, with a nurse at her side. Nikki felt weak. Brad wasn't in the room. Neither was Lillian. She looked at the nurse and asked, "How is the baby?"

The nurse smiled. "Your baby is doing okay."

A flood of tears drained from Nikki's eyes. Relief washed over her, bringing peace into her heart.

My baby is okay.

Both of them survived.

♥

## A Spiritual Message from Lillian Bay.

*In this world, I will experience joy in so many special ways. A gentle wind to help with my breathing. The sound of my voice giggling for the first time. A unique star glowing in the clear night sky.*

*God whispered to me that every moment in life should be treated as special. He told me that if I could find a way to smile, laugh, and enjoy each precious day, then others would learn from my example.*

## Lillian Bay, Medical Report

Date: November 12th, 2009

Notes:

- Evaluation needed of neck mass, extending to her chin. Brad and Nikki Beatty are at Lillian's bedside during consultation.
- Patient was delivered at 39-weeks due to neck mass found during pregnancy.
- Doctor had planned to keep the infant attached to the placenta while airway was evaluated.
  However, the cord ruptured during delivery and had to be clamped.
- Infant transferred to NICU.
- Mother reports no past exposure to prescription medication, drugs, alcohol, smoking, fever, bleeding, or rashes during pregnancy.
- Diagnosis of patient: Most likely an isolated Cystic Hygroma.

Lillian Bay Beatty

# SHE'S BEAUTIFUL

*"The Lord said, 'I will give you a new heart and put a new spirit within you.'"*

**~ Ezekiel 36:26**

Nurse Scott was tending to Lillian at NICU while Brad gazed at his baby girl. Her hair was matted with sweat. Her skin pale and body weak with exhaustion. Lillian had fought so hard during her birth. Despite the prognosis and the lack of air getting into her tiny lungs, Lillian kept on breathing.

Brad watched as tubes and wires were connected to his child. He forced a tired grin, taking pictures of Lillian in her yellow diaper.

It's going to be okay.

She alive. She's fighting.

Lillian will keep on breathing.

None of us will give up on her.

Brad swallowed back his tears, thinking that his little girl still had a long, tough road ahead of her. But no matter what, he was going to do everything in his power to give Lillian a chance at life.

♥

Brad was still a new husband. Now, he was a new father. His little girl was being taken care of in NICU, while his wife was being transported through an underground tunnel to Bayfront Medical Center.

His family was split into separate hospitals. Brad understood the reasons why his daughter had to be taken care of in one place, while his wife was in another, receiving her own special care. Still, it was agonizing as both a husband, and a father.

Brad was on his way to visit Nikki, carrying a cooler of spare vials of blood that had been donated, because she had lost so much. He gripped the cooler, picked up his pace, anxious to see her.

His thoughts drifted.

Is there anything else I can be doing to help my family?

♥

The next day, Nikki was still being given morphine for the pain. Regardless of how she felt, Nikki wanted to see her sweet Lillian Bay. In order for that to happen, Nikki would have to be transported from Bayfront Medical Center to All Children's Hospital. It would be difficult and dangerous for Nikki, because she was still recovering.

"I want to see my baby," Nikki demanded. "Take me to see her."

The doctor conceded and gave permission for Brad to transport Nikki in a wheelchair to NICU at All Children's Hospital.

♥

Before anyone could enter the room, they had to be scrubbed and sanitized. In addition, Brad and Nikki had to wear a sterile gown and cap. After they were prepped, the nurse buzzed them into the room. Brad gently pushed Nikki forward in the wheelchair and approached the bed.

Their little baby girl was asleep. Brad and Nikki looked past the wires. They did not hear the sounds of machines keeping her alive. Instead, they saw their beautiful daughter sleeping. They envisioned what Lillian was dreaming.

Clear skies.

Warm ocean.

Playing at the beach.

A cool sea breeze.

Laughing. Breathing. Living.

"Look what we made," Nikki cried, touching Lillian's delicate fingers. Tears of joy welled up in Nikki's eyes. "She's beautiful."

Brad gazed at his family. It seemed so long ago when Nikki was just thirty-two weeks pregnant and they were given the bad news about their baby. That dark moment had turned into this perfect light.

There is a black spot on your baby's neck. "No," Brad thought to himself. "She is beautiful."

There is a mass on your baby's lower jaw. "It does not matter . . . she is magnificent."

We are unfamiliar with this kind of problem. "God understands the problem and has a solution."

This is a rare condition. "Lillian Bay is rare indeed; an inspiration to all other children."

She has Cystic Hygroma, something that most doctors have not encountered. "Lillian will triumph over the disease. She will prove to the world that sickness cannot steal a second of her joy."

Her chances are not good. "We do not believe in chance. We believe in hope, faith, love, and wisdom. We believe in fighting with everything we have and everything that we do not have."

You are going to need many prayers. "God has already answered those prayers."

Brad knelt down next to Nikki and his baby girl. Despite everything, they were all together for the first time.

They were a family.

♥

Gifts poured in for the nursing staff, sent by stores from Boca Grande. The nurses received beach purses, note cards, candles, scarves, and other items.

This would become a common theme of Boca Grande. The residents and businesses wanted to show support for Brad, Nikki, and Lillian, along with all of the people that worked endless hours for Lillian.

Boca Grande became an example of a community with an endless amount of love, provision, and a passion to help.

♥

Over the next two days, Lillian was kept inside an incubator. She had a heart monitor hooked up to her foot and two leads on her chest. Unfortunately, Brad and Nikki could not hold her. Instead, they put their fingers through the glass, barely touching her little hand.

Then on November 13th, they were able to hold their baby girl for the first time. They felt her warmth and strength. They placed family photos around Lillian, surrounding her with love. There was even a picture of the fourth member of their family.

A chocolate Lab named Hannah.

Together as a family, it seemed as if God were saying, "You showed faith in Me...here is your reward."

♥

**A Spiritual Message from Lillian Bay.**

*God loves us so much and gives us so many chances to love Him back. Being with family in a moment of peace, we can block out the world and think only of love . . . Love . . . LOVE!*

## Lillian Bay, Medical Report

Date: November 17th, 2009

Notes:

- Multiple cyst-like lesions are seen with fluid.
- An endotracheal tube has been coursed through the patient's mouth during incubation. Airway is limited.

Lillian Bay Beatty

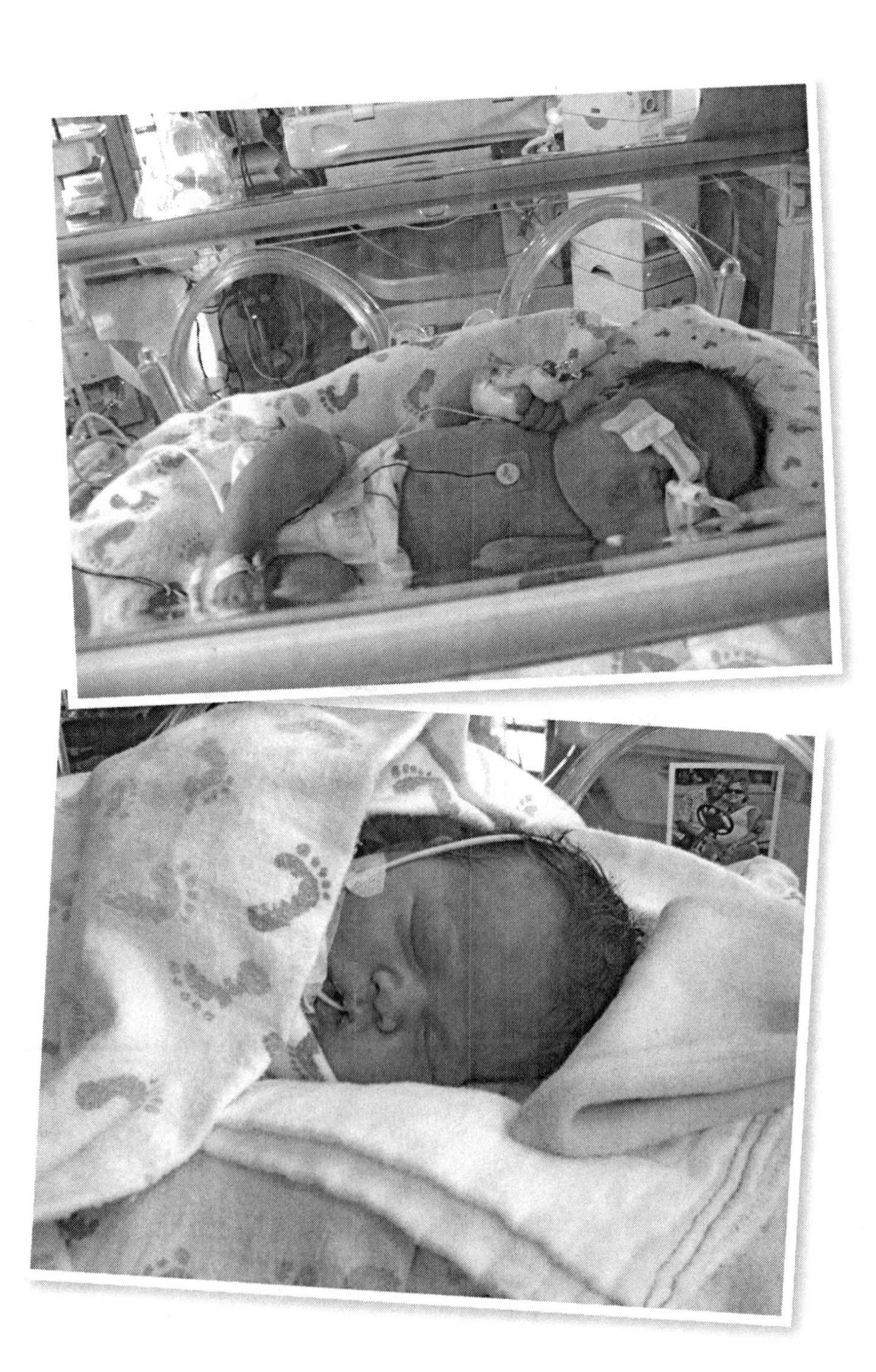

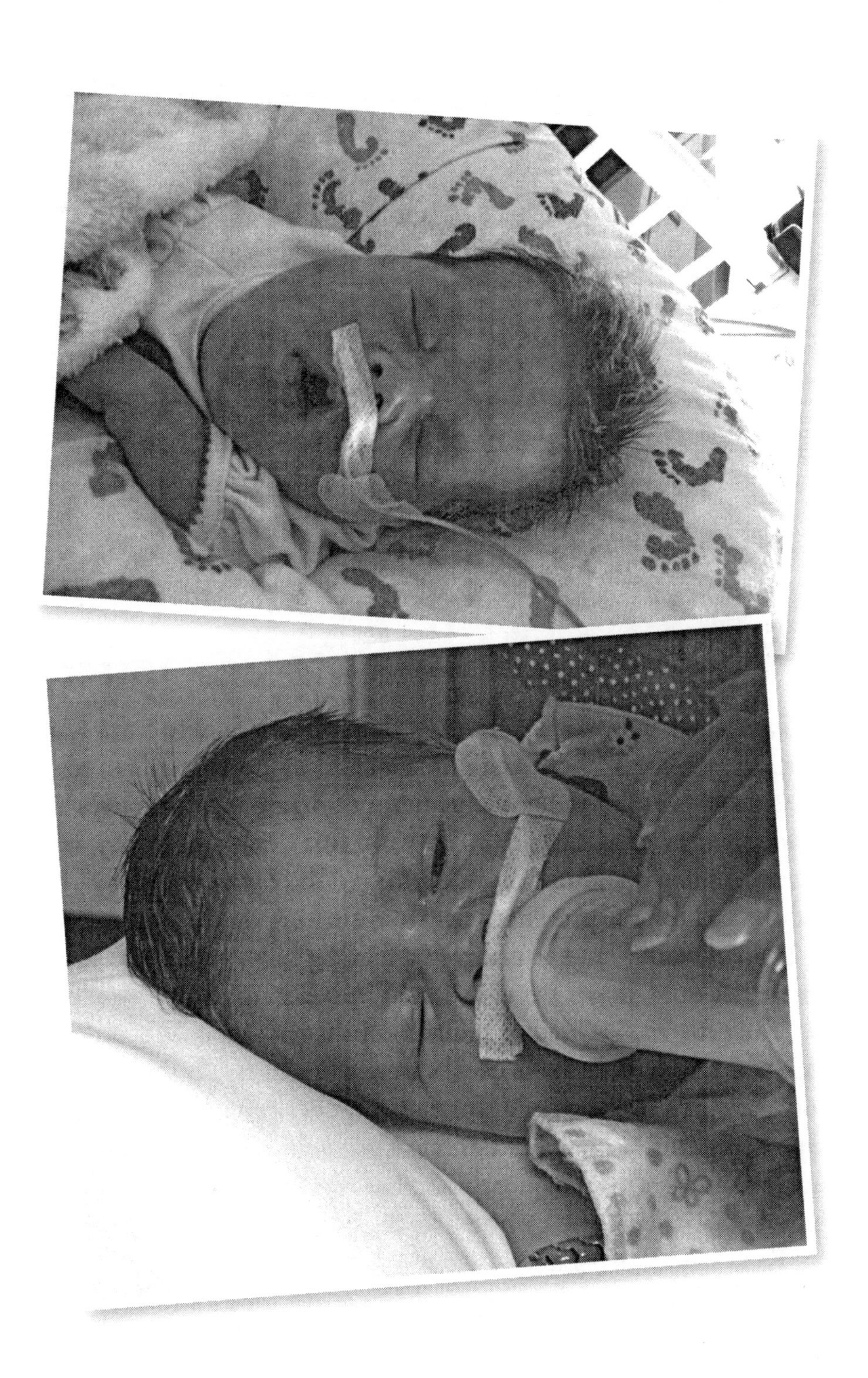

# Miracles Happen

*"A voice from heaven said, 'God will wipe away every tear from their eyes; there shall be no more death, no sorrow, no crying... There shall be no more pain.'"*

**~ Revelation 22:4**

Lillian had to be trained differently than other babies to learn how to suck on a bottle. Brad and Nikki started by turning Lillian to the side and resting the bottle by her mouth, along with nurses doing therapy to assist Lillian. They did this three times a day, even though Lillian could not drink anything. The Hygroma in her mouth and tongue prevented her from sucking on the bottle.

Lillian would have to eat from a feeding tube, which was placed inside her nose, down her throat, and into her stomach.

The tube was secured to Lillian's cheeks with tape. When the tape was removed, Lillian's cheeks were a bright red, but not the rosy glow of a healthy child. Instead, her cheeks had the glow from tape being constantly placed on her skin and removed. Also, the nurse would have to frequently suction out the excess fluid in her lungs, which was done by bringing the fluid up through the tube.

Each breath that Lillian took was a struggle. Her mouth made a soft squeaking sound as she fought to retrieve even the smallest pocket of air. And with each breath, Lillian's eyes became wide, struggling to live.

Brad and Nikki took turns holding their baby, whispering, "Are you okay, honey?" They would look away from Lillian, attempting to hide their own sorrow. Their hearts shredded, listening as Lillian used each second of her life to tug in a critical, faint breath.

♥

Surgery was needed when Lillian was three weeks old to put in a trachea and a belly-feeding peg that will hang about one foot off the baby's stomach. The peg is problematical and challenging, because the pump can easily burst, which causes syrup looking fluid to drain all over the baby. To solve this problem, another surgery was needed to connect a G-Tube, which was easier to work and has fewer problems.

Brad and Nikki had adjusted to the routine of visiting with their daughter. Before each visit, they had to go through the sterilization process and put on sterile clothes. Nikki healed well and certainly deserved the title, "Wonderful Mother," after all she had gone through.

More tests were being done on Lillian to determine how she should be treated. In fact, no one really knew exactly why this happened to Lillian, or what will occur in the next few weeks.

Six days after Lillian was born, she was moved to a normal crib in NICU. This made her more accessible to Brad and Nikki.

Meanwhile, the doctors continued to search for answers.

♥

Brad and Nikki soon realized that they were not alone in their fight to save Lillian.

Brad's best friend, Heavy Duty, took care of the house while they were gone. He mowed the grass and did odd jobs around the home to fix it up. "It seemed like Heavy Duty was sent here to help me during my most difficult time," Brad said. "I don't know what I would have done without him."

Family and friends continued to visit. No longer were these just photographs in a hospital room. Lillian was able to meet everyone in person. She was surrounded by love and prayers.

♥

The administrative employees at the Boca Grande Fire Department decided that instead of exchanging Christmas gifts, they would use the money that would have been spent on each other and give it to a needy cause.

As Christmas approached in December 2009, they agreed that Lillian Bay would be their choice for that year. The team of firefighters wanted to contribute as well. They donated all the gift cards that they had just received from others and added more presents. Then, the firefighters climbed into the fire truck with the cards and presents and went searching for Brad in his UPS truck.

Sirens blared, echoing throughout Boca Grande.

The firefighters located Brad and delivered him the gifts.

♥

## Lillian Bay, Medical Report

Date: December 1st, 2009

Notes:

- Airway obstruction, predominately caused by Cystic Hygroma.
- Emergent neck mass.
- Suction required every 2 - 4 hours and once overnight during feed to prevent vomiting.
- Alternative/Supplemental feedings required.
- Imperative to monitor ear function and loss of hearing to determine whether it is medically manageable.
- Endoscopy Tube placement.

Lillian Bay Beatty

## Lillian Bay, Medical Report

Date: December 14th, 2009

Notes:

- Life support lines are in place.
- Mild lung disease.
- After risks and alternatives were discussed with Brad and Nikki Beatty, along with consent obtained, the patient was brought to the Special Procedures Unit at All Children's Hospital for endoscopic evaluation.
- Risks include bleeding perforation, infection, mucosal hematoma, allergic reaction to sedation medications, and respiratory depression.
- The endoscope was passed through the mouth, into the esophagus, and into the stomach.
- The area was then infiltrated with 1% Xylocaine, then a 25-gauge needle was passed into the stomach.
- The needle came through the skin, into the stomach to mark the site where the PEG was going to be done.

Lillian Bay Beatty

## Lillian Bay, Medical Report

Date: December 14th, 2009

Notes:

- An incision was then made in the skin, only at that site.
- A 14-gauge Angiocath was passed through the incision, into the stomach.
- The suture material, forceps, and endoscope were then pulled out through the esophagus and out through the mouth.
- A 14-French PEG tube was tied to the suture material and pulled back into the stomach, through the abdominal wall.
- Lillian Bay tolerated the procedure well and was sent back to the recovery room in satisfactory condition.

Lillian Bay Beatty

## Lillian Bay, Medical Report

Date: December 21st, 2009

Notes:

- Life support lines are in place.
- Newly inserted tracheostomy tube.
- Trachea air column is somewhat narrowed.
- Bronchovascular ill definition is seen.
- The neck mass has a large ball of soft tissues projecting to the left of the patients head.
- A PICC catheter has been placed in the upper left extremity.
- Slightly less prominence of the heart.
- Enteric tube in place with its tip overlying the stomach.
- Lungs are well expanded and aerated.
- Bones are normal size and aligned.
- Fullness of the neck, consistent with malformation. (Cystic Lymphangioma.)

Lillian Bay Beatty

## Lillian Bay, Medical Report

Date: December 28th, 2009

Notes:

- Mucous plugging in association with infectious lung disease such as bronchiolitis.

Lillian Bay Beatty

♥

The bills piled up. With two house payments, along with maintenance, Brad and Nikki would not be able to survive. They needed to sell one of the homes.

The decision was difficult, because the house they lived in now was in good shape, but more sellable on the market. Brad's house was still under repair due to damage from Hurricane Charley. No one would purchase that house under its current condition.

Should they live in the house they were in and try to survive with both payments, while continuing to fall behind with Lillian's medical bills?

Or should they move into the house with construction problems, which will be harder to live in and even more difficult to take care of Lillian's medical needs?

In addition, something else weighed on their minds. Brad and Nikki had worked so hard on Lillian's bedroom to have it ready for when she came home. It was furnished and decorated to perfection. Lillian's bedroom was a symbol of Brad and Nikki's faith; their daughter would survive and sleep in this room.

Brad and Nikki decided that their only choice was to sell the house they were living in, then move into the other house and fix it up the best they could.

Despite the market, and with the help of Gasparilla Properties on Boca Grande, Brad and Nikki were able to sell the house in quick fashion. After the sale of the house, they made a $350 profit.

With a heavy heart, Brad took apart Lillian's bedroom and moved everything into the other house.

♥

Each time Brad stayed with Nikki and Lillian at the hospital, it had been difficult for him to leave. Nevertheless, he had to keep working. His family needed the money and the medical insurance.

The days at UPS began to get longer. At night, he had to work on the house. The weekends were the only time he could visit his family.

Nikki had made a full recovery and was released from the hospital. Just like Brad, it was extremely difficult for Nikki to go home without her baby. Nothing was going to keep her away. She drove back to the hospital every morning, which took over an hour and a half. Each night, she would make the long trip home.

On the weekends, Brad and Nikki stayed at the Ronald McDonald House, located next to the hospital. The room was free, but they had to wash their own sheets and had extra duties like wiping down tables, or vacuuming. Since their money was tight, they were thankful for the Ronald McDonald House and gladly did the chores.

Gas prices continued to rise. The trips to All Children's Hospital began to drain what was left in their bank account. And because Nikki missed so much work, she had to leave her job at the Boca Beacon and file for unemployment.

Christmas season approached, giving Brad some much-needed overtime. However, it would also mean spending less time with his wife and daughter.

During the busy season, just about everyone on Boca Grande received a package. As he delivered the boxes, people continued to show their support and say things like, "We have been praying for Lillian and your family." Brad felt like the entire Island of Boca Grande was literally in the back of his UPS truck. They were with him on every stop, every delivery, and every step he took.

Brad worked hard, yet it was not enough to distract him from the emotional fears that plagued him daily.

Lillian is still sick.

They were rarely together as a family.

The house needed more repairs.

Their vehicle was breaking down.

Medical bills arrived each day.

He missed Nikki.

He missed his daughter.

Then something happened. It was a moment that Brad would look back on as a turning point in his life, bringing him closer to God.

Brad had delivered a package to Gasparilla Properties and hurried back to his truck. Just before he stepped up into the truck, he noticed something on the metal grate floor. He leaned closer to get a better look, making sure it was real.

On the floor was a magnet. He had no idea where it came from, or how it got there. Brad could not move, still gazing at the magnet. Chills ran down his arms and his heart swelled with the spirit of God. Tears began to moisten his eyes.

The magnet had two words on it..."Miracles Happen."

♥

## A Spiritual Message from Lillian Bay.

*When you are down to your last dollar, look at it carefully.*
*If you do this, then you will see the words,*
*"In God We Trust."*

# GOING HOME

*"Your children will come back home. I, the Lord, have spoken."*

**~ Jeremiah 31:17**

Prior to bringing Lillian home, Brad and Nikki were given extensive training by the entire staff, along with Nurse Bev Fann, someone that they had grown fond of and considered a friend.

They were taught how to feed Lillian with the food pump. Also, they were taught how to use the heart monitor machine and the suction machine. Finally, they were trained on how to use the emergency "Go-Bag," with infant CPR and tracheostomy changes.

Brad and Nikki wanted to feel delighted that they were bringing their daughter home for the first time. Nevertheless, they were terrified. It was their turn to take care of Lillian. Nurse Bev would not be there to help. Doctors would not be an emergency button away from coming to Lillian's rescue.

They would not be secure in the walls of All Children's Hospital.

Carefully they loaded Lillian into their family vehicle. Brad drove, while Nikki sat in the backseat with Lillian. Brad gripped the steering wheel, eyes darting in every direction. The pressure of driving a UPS truck with thousands of dollars in packages, delivering them safely to their destination, was nothing compared to this single trip home.

What if something happened to Lillian? What would they do?

What if another car hit them?

What if it started raining and the roads became slick?

What if they were caught in a traffic jam? Would Lillian be okay?

What if Lillian stopped breathing?

Brad recalled asking the doctor before they left the hospital, "Can we save Lillian if something happens to her on the way home?" The question repeated in his mind.

Can we save Lillian if something happens to her on the way home?

Lillian was hooked up to a heart monitor, about the size of a lunchbox. If Lillian's heart slowed, an alarm would go off. It detected episodes, choking, and heart failure. Brad and Nikki took CPR classes at All Children's Hospital, but prayed the alarm would not go off during their trip home.

Even with all this preparation, Brad felt like he was trapped inside the vehicle with his family. Nikki's voice was cracked with nervousness. They had gone through so much to save Lillian's life. A simple ninety-minute drive seemed like another life-threatening obstacle they would have to overcome.

♥

When Brad pulled into the driveway, it was as if he could breathe again. The medical equipment was being dropped off and setup in their bedroom next to the crib, along with the misting collar, which provides sterile water to keep the trachea moist.

Brad and Nikki wanted to keep their eye on Lillian at all times. They attempted to recall everything they were taught in the hospital.

Are we using the machines correctly?

Is every wire in the correct place?

It was impossible to get any rest. The Apnea Monitor continued to beep, as if trying to gain Brad and Nikki's attention. The leads kept falling off because they were not sticky enough. The belly connection had a leaking problem.

Meanwhile, Lillian was given silver nitrates to slow down the growth at the union of the belly tube. Sometimes, the nitrate would burn her stomach. A persistent infection in Lillian's trachea, along with a recurring pneumonia and aspirating a couple of times a week, increased the amount of hospital trips for Brad and Nikki, while decreasing their opportunities for sleep.

Each time Brad returned to work, he experienced more helplessness. Two things kept him moving forward:

Paycheck.

Medical insurance.

Suddenly, their world spun out of control . . .

♥

"I'm almost at your house," Brad's mother said to Nikki on the phone. "I'll give you a hand today while Brad's at work."

Nikki was exhausted, but could not leave to go grocery shopping. All she wanted right now was caffeine. "I'm sorry to ask, but can you get me a Coke?"

"No problem. I can head back to the grocery store. I'll just be a few minutes." Brad's mother turned the car around. An elderly woman drove to a stop sign, braked, then stepped on the gas, colliding into Brad's mother.

The vehicles smashed together with jarring force.

Metal crunched and glass shattered.

The car spun and then went airborne, flipping over two and half times before landing on the passenger's side. Brad's mother had soft tissue injuries and severe bruises on her chest, legs, stomach, caused by the seatbelt and steering wheel as the car flipped over several times.

A string of terrible events began to affect Brad and Nikki's outside world.

Brad's grandmother passed away.

Brad's aunt and uncle passed away.

A good friend of Brad and Nikki's died of Lou Gehrigs Disease.

They received news that one of the nurses from All Children's Hospital in which they had become good friends with, Bev Fann, passed away. At her funeral, Brad and Nikki held Lillian and said a few words, letting everyone know how special she was to them.

Problems with Lillian seemed to become worse. She had stopped breathing several times. EMT's were called. Each time, they were able to stabilize her.

Adding to the difficulties, Lillian continued to get clogs and infections in her trachea.

Brad and Nikki desperately needed an in-house nursing staff that could work in at least two shifts: eight hours during the day and eight hours in the evening. Their request was being considered.

Between the mental and physical strain of taking care of Lillian, the escalating medical bills, and the passing of their family and friends, it was difficult for Brad and Nikki to believe things would get any better.

That is when the arguments started. Nikki felt that Brad was not home enough to help. They fought about money, bills, and their house that was falling apart. Brad's temper was short and Nikki's patience was nonexistent.

Their endurance as a husband and wife began to run its course . . .

# For One Child...
# For All Children

*"Creating healthy tomorrows . . .*
*for one child . . . for all children!"*

**~ All Children's Hospital**

All Children's Hospital prepared to move a few blocks away into a more state-of-the-art building. The timing could not have been better for Lillian. Some of the upgrades would be:

- Military Sized Helicopter Pad.
- Twenty-Eight-Bed Pediatric Care Unit.
- Pediatric Heart Center.
- Ninety-Seven-Bed Neonatal Intensive Care Unit.
- Twelve State-of-the-art Operating Suites.
- Pediatric Clinical Research Center.
- Four Playrooms designed for children with different abilities.
- Gigantic Cafeteria!

Lillian would receive the best and latest medical treatments. Most of all, it would be an environment that helped patients and families feel comfortable during their stay.

All Children's Hospital prepared to transport the patients and staff. When the nurses arrived in the new hospital, a blanket was sewn by a volunteer, framed and hung on the wall for every parent and child to see. The blanket represented survival, love, and devotion. It offered hope to worried parents and children.

A symbol that everything will become new.

♥

## A Spiritual Message from Lillian Bay.

*It is hard to be happy when things are not so great. But there are reasons why we should be happy today. God is with us! And God knows what He is doing!*

*From my little space here, I cannot see everything that is going on all around me. I can only understand this tiny piece of the world that I live in. I just have to trust that God will handle everything else.*

*God placed a blanket of hope around me, then used that blanket to nurture other children, comforting them with His care and love.*

## Lillian Bay, Medical Report

Date: Janurary 19th, 2010

Notes:

- Acute choking episode that resulted in brief apneic event.
- Viral upper respiratory infection.
- Trach became clogged and an emergency trach was needed.
- EMS was called and patient was taken to Peace River Emergency Center, stabilized, then transferred to All Children's Hospital for further observation.
- Day of admission, patient had a coughing event and secondary choking episode; became cyanotic in the lips and face.
- Recommended change in formula.
- Skin Team was consulted and they recommended PolyMem dressing under the G-tube.
- Patient is awake and alert. Airway is clear.
- Twenty-Four hour home nursing was requested by parents, however, denied by private insurance.

Lillian Bay Beatty

## Lillian Bay, Medical Report

Date: Janurary 27th, 2010

Notes:

- Increased secretions from the trach tube and oral cavity. Parents claim the trach has needed suction that is more frequent.
- Patient vomiting mucus.
- Mild coarseness of the lung. This can be seen in the setting of chronic lung disease.
- Cystic Hygroma has grown in the last week, primarily in the floor of the mouth and tongue.
- Recommend supportive care and wait until further treatments and procedures can be administered.

Lillian Bay Beatty

## Lillian Bay, Medical Report

Date: February 10th, 2010

Notes:

- MRI performed, causing a spike in the patient's temperature.
- Modest improvement in neck area. Cystic components appear to have decreased in size somewhat.
- PSA Home Nursing has been reconsidered and approved. Home nursing is to start immediately.

Lillian Bay Beatty

An account in Lillian Bay's name had been set up at the bank for donations to help for medical expenses.

## Donations into the Lillian Bay Medical Fund

$250 on March 5th, 2010
Nine more donations were deposited from residents and businesses of Boca Grande

## Lillian Bay, Medical Report

Date: March 14th, 2010

Notes:

- Patient has non-productive cough, difficulty breathing, and fever.
- Increased secretions by the trach.
- Severe respiratory distress.
- Patient was rushed to Fawcett Memorial Emergency Room and started on oxygen, then transferred to All Children's Hospital for further evaluation.
- Social history questions were conducted on parents. There is pet exposure. No contacts with anyone that is sick. Mother also reports that she washes her hands constantly.
- Patient will be given respiratory treatments and monitored closely.

Lillian Bay Beatty

## Donations into the Lillian Bay Medical Fund

$50 on March 16th, 2010:
Four more donations were deposited from
residents and businesses of Boca Grande

## Lillian Bay, Medical Report

Date: March 18th, 2010

Notes:

- Tracheostomy tube and gastrostomy tube remain in place.
- Reports of cough, vomiting, and pneumonia.
- The lungs are clear and stable in their appearance as compared to the prior exam from January 26th, 2010.

Lillian Bay Beatty

## Donations into the Lillian Bay medical Fund

$50 on March 30th, 2010

$200 on march 31st, 2010

$390 on April 2nd, 2010

$250 on April 5th, 2010

Forty-One more donations were deposited from residents and businesses of Boca Grande

# Community & Love

*"I will not be silent until she is saved...and her victory shines like a torch in the night."*

**~ Isaiah 61:1**

The Cystic Hygroma had grown, wrapping around Lillian's mouth and throat, making it extremely difficult for Lillian to breathe. The trach needed to be suctioned constantly, which meant, either Brad or Nikki had to be at Lillian's bedside at all times.

Thankfully, Nikki's mother spent many hours at the house so that Brad and Nikki could get some sleep.

Brad and Nikki had to create a stock room at the house for Lillian's medical boxes. There wasn't much space, but they had little choice. Also, they had either problems with too many supplies, or always running out of supplies. They were constantly on the phone, trying to solve this never-ending dilemma.

Despite problems with the medical supplier, Brad was more than satisfied with his insurance. Without private insurance, Lillian would not have received anything. Brad wished that all children could be blessed with such terrific health coverage, giving every child the best chance to survive a major illness.

In spite of this, out-of-pocket medical expenses were going beyond what could realistically be paid. Threatening letters from hospital bookkeepers arrived daily. Brad and Nikki did not want to ignore their bills; however, there simply was not enough money.

In response to Brad and Nikki's hardships, on April 18th, a spaghetti dinner and raffle to benefit Lillian Bay was organized by the residents of Boca Grande to be held at the Crowninshield Community House. The event was sponsored by Nat Italiano and the Boca Beacon Newspaper.

The Boca Beacon was doing everything possible to keep Lillian's story on the front page, so that the entire island would know about the fundraiser and participate. Also, North Port Magazine did an article on Lillian Bay with her picture on the cover and even used some of their paid radio airtime to advertise the event.

Joy Wyman, a resident of Boca Grande and a person that organizes volunteers in the community to make desserts for fundraisers, talked about Boca Grande. "This is a very special fundraiser for the Beatty family and their precious daughter Lillian. Where else does a whole island sit down to eat spaghetti and help their community?"

That statement could not have been more accurate. Even though most of the residents had headed back north for spring season, 385 adults and 23 children attended the spaghetti dinner and raised $12,000 for Lillian's medical expenses.

The event also included prayers, words of encouragement, and many uplifting hugs.

$2,500 was raised from the 50/50 raffle. The winners of the raffle, David and Nancy Gaffney were notified, but they requested the money be used for the additional medical expenses.

The principal at The Island School on Boca Grande, Rosa Rumos, had this to say, "It's so important to help every family that lives and works here, especially when the help is needed for a child."

At the end of the event, Brad stood up in front of everyone, tears misting his eyes, and said, "Boca Grande . . . wow." Choked with emotion, Brad continued. "You have all shown that Boca Grande is a very loving place. You should be so proud of your community." He paused, looking at his daughter, tears streaming down his face. "Lillian Bay shows us how to live for every moment...She has inspired me."

Brad took in a few deep breaths to compose himself. "I'm not saying it's going to be easy to overcome this, but it will be worth it." Brad's voice was shaken, yet he fought to remain strong. He wiped the tears from his eyes and said, "We just need a miracle."

♥

**Donations into the Lillian Bay Medical Fund**

$3,015 on April 19th, 2010

$1,000 on April 26th, 2010

Twenty more donations were deposited from residents and businesses of Boca Grande

♥

## Lillian Bay, Medical Report

Date: April 30th, 2010

Notes:

- Patient has severe swelling in her face.
  Emergency surgery is needed to drain the fluid.
- The patient was brought into the operating room and placed on the operating table in the supine position.
- After general anesthesia was induced, the right neck was prepped and draped in the usual sterile fashion.
- Incision was open with a scalpel. Hematoma was evacuated from the wound and the wound was profusely irrigated.
- A flat 10 French Jackson-Pratt drain was then inserted through a separate stab incision and the wound was closed in layers.
- The patient was taken to the recovery room in satisfactory condition.

Lillian Bay Beatty

## Lillian Bay, Medical Report

Date: May 6th, 2010

Notes:

- Patient is having problems with drain care and the wound from surgery on April 30th has developed a fluid collection.
- Day 1, drain was kept on wall suction.
- Day 2, leakage discovered around drain.
- Day 3, the patient was taken back to the operating room to have the drain removed and a new one put in its place.
- Day 4, no events, or problems.
- Day 5, the drain once again had to be replaced. Patient developed a burn on the abdomen from silver nitrate used to cauterize G-tube. Skin Care Team was consulted and treated patient.
- Days 8 & 9, drain had been removed and patient was monitored for twenty-four hours. Drain had significantly decreased.
- Day 10, patient in stable condition and was discharged to go home.

Lillian Bay Beatty

♥

## Donations into the Lillian Bay Medical Fund

$20 on May 7th, 2010

Twelve more donations were deposited from residents and businesses of Boca Grande

♥

On May 9th, 2010, a friend of Nikki's mother, Darlene, along with the executives at Harpoon Harry's, Ron, Chris, and Tammy, organized a fundraising event at Harpoon Harry's in Punta Gorda, Florida. In addition to the terrific menu, there was live music and a 50/50 raffle. Darlene and the staff at Harpoon Harry's received praise from both Brad and Nikki for the outstanding job that they had done with the event.

Plenty of Boca Grande residents and businesses donated items to raise money. For example, the Gasparilla Inn gave away a two-night stay and a free round of golf. Tarpon Realty auctioned off a week vacation in two different homes located on the island. Underwater Fish Light gave away an ocean light that is used to attract fish. The owner, John Molle, had been ill at that time, but still found the strength to donate his time and treasure.

Five doctors from Faucet Hospital made significant donations. Local fisherman gave charters away. And many UPS employees attended to show their support.

In the past, Brad ordered various items from Bustin Skateboards. He had never met the owners, but decided to email them and ask if they would make a donation. Bustin Skateboards agreed to send a beautiful wooden skateboard deck.

Originally, the deck was supposed to be auctioned off. It was placed next to the raffle tickets near the sign-in area. For some reason, the first guest that arrived signed their name on the skateboard. Then another and another. In fact, every person that attended the event signed his or her name on the skateboard.

Brad decided not to auction it off. Instead, he put the skateboard in Lillian's room as a reminder of how many people supported and cared for her.

In total, the event raised $13,000 for Lillian's medical expenses.

When it was time to clean up, Brad stayed behind to help. A waitress, Amanda McCorkle, had been working during the event, approached Brad and handed him a wad of cash. "Here you go."

"What's this?" Brad asked.

"It's to help your daughter." Amanda then smiled and said, "This is all of the tips that I earned today."

♥

## A Spiritual Message from Lillian Bay.

*How can we, shine like a torch? It's easy. When you see someone that needs help, give them a smile, a hug, and words to cheer them up. When you give to others, then you give to Jesus.*

*Faith is something that we need, but also something that we must share. When you give and help others, you shine like a torch!*

# Never Left Alone

*"The greatest love a person can have for his friends is to give his life for them."*

**~ John 15:13**

Larry Frazer, also known as "Heavy Duty," lived in South Gulf Cove, which is about twenty minutes from Boca Grande. Brad had also delivered in that area when things were slow at UPS. And just like Boca Grande, he formed close relationships, especially with Heavy Duty.

To keep Brad sane, Heavy Duty suggested that Brad help fix up old cars. He could then sell them to raise additional money for medical expenses. Also, while Brad spent long hours at the hospital, he could research and purchase parts that they needed for the cars.

A few of the vehicles they worked on were a 74' VW Karmann Ghia and a 1920 Speedster.

Heavy Duty was always just a phone call away if Brad needed anything. He was a blessing for Brad and never asked for anything in return.

♥

Anyone can be left alone and forced to struggle with problems without a hint of guidance, or wisdom. Brad could have been left alone, but his character brought him closer to the people on Boca Grande.

When Brad struggled with Lillian's health and continued losing the battle in his marriage, Archie Hager became Brad's spiritual friend. Not because Archie felt sorry for Brad, or because Archie wanted to feel good about himself. Instead, it was a calling on a deeper level that mere words could not describe.

Archie, COO of Hager Company, St. Louis, Missouri, first heard what was happening from his brother Rusty, CEO of Hager Company. Rusty brought together the community to support Brad and talk him through this difficult time using encouraging words and prayers of hope.

Personally, Archie spoke with Brad just about every day, even if it was for only ten minutes. He formed a close relationship with Brad and became his mentor. Whether Archie was on Boca Grande or in St. Louis on business, he stayed in touch with Brad. Wanting something in return was not part of Archie's reasoning.

People should not have to handle problems alone.

Brad needed care.

He needed someone that would just listen.

Doing the right thing, but not taking credit for it.

Anyone can be a friend, but not everyone can be a true friend.

Archie knew about the endless medical bills. However, money would not solve all of Brad's problems. There was not a clear path to saving Lillian, or saving his marriage. Brad needed spiritual guidance.

He needed a friend.

♥

So many other people became close to Brad, uplifting him with a kind word or a frequent prayer. Brad admitted that he was far from perfect and needed friends for encouragement. He made friends at several churches. Friends on Boca Grande. Friends at UPS.

They did for him, what he sometimes could not do for himself.

Strength.

Inspiration.

Hope.

Wisdom.

Love.

♥

## Donations into the Lillian Bay Medical Fund

$10,800 on May 11th, 2010

$1,300 on May 11th, 2010

$1,540 on May 15th, 2010

Twenty-Six more donations were deposited from residents and businesses of Boca Grande

♥

Jennifer Burch, owner of Palm on the Park, which is a Lilly Pulitzer Signature Store on Boca Grande, wanted to do something to help Brad and his family. Jennifer, along with the other employees of Palm on the Park understood that Brad has excellent insurance through UPS, but there were still out of pocket expenses, days of work missed, and sometimes more money going out than coming in.

They just wanted to help.

Palm on the Park offered two hundred Lilly Pulitzer silk scarves as a fundraiser. Each person that made a Lillian Bay donation would receive one of those prized scarves. Soon after, Palm on the Park was able to deposit $5,000 into the bank account that was set up to help the family to assist with their bills.

Kris Boyden, manager of Palm on the Park said, "We were all so proud that we were able to help make a difference."

Whenever Brad would bring Lillian into the store, it was a bright spot in their day. Even with all of Lillian's difficulties, she would still laugh and play like any other child. The employees would dress up Lillian in different outfits that they had in the store.

"It takes a village to raise a child," Kris said, using the famous quote. "All of us on Boca Grande are Lilly's village."

Even when Brad would make a delivery in the store, he would update them on the kind of day Lillian was having. Palm on the Park is just one of hundreds of stops that Brad makes during his UPS route and everyone received the same update. When Lillian was having a good day, it was easy for Brad to share the information.

When Lillian was having a bad day, the repeated update was much more difficult.

Palm on the Park, along with the other businesses and residents on Boca Grande, became Brad's cheerleaders. They applauded his efforts, spoke words of faith, and prayed with thankful and encouraging words.

## A Spiritual Message from Lillian Bay.

*Write a thank you letter to a friend. Send a friend a card to show that you are thinking of them. Draw a picture for your friend. Help your friend with a tough choice they have to make. Listen to your friend. Pray for your friend. Most of all, think about why you became friends. "A friend loves at all times."*

**~ Proverbs 17:17**

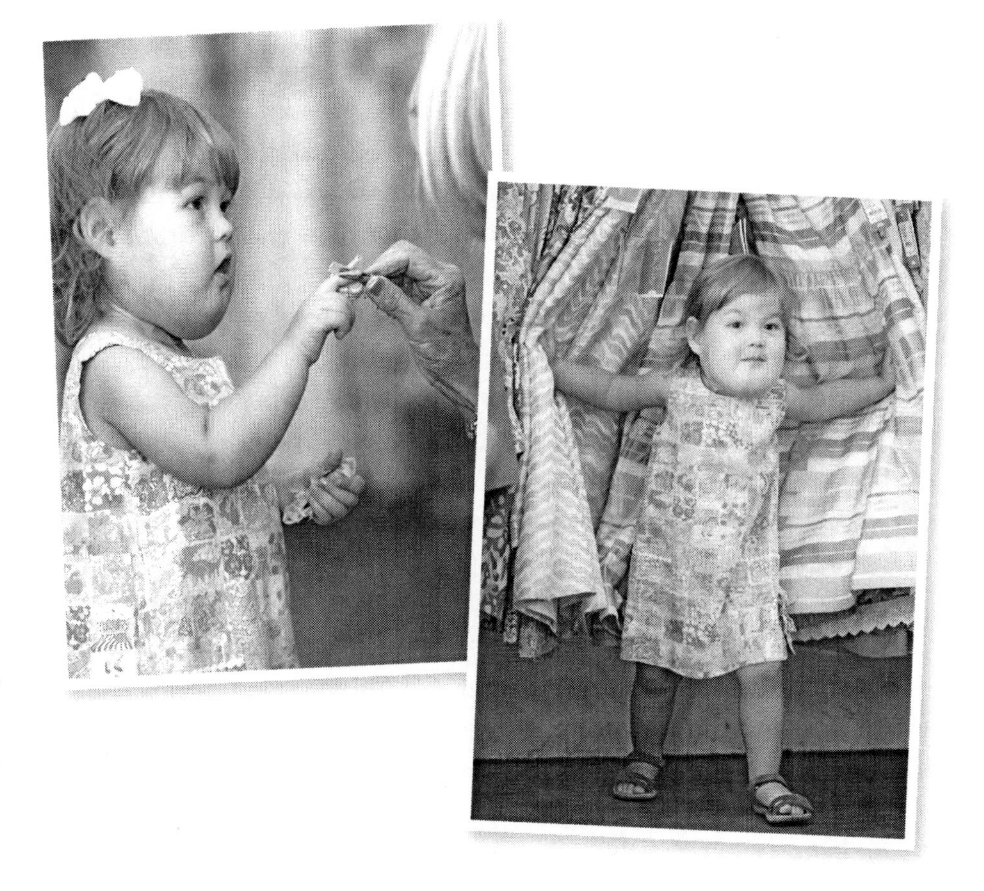

# Beating the Odds

*"Give her credit for all she does.*
*She deserves the respect of everyone."*

**~ Proverbs 31:31**

Another surgery had originally been planned for Lillian as soon as she weighed twenty pounds. In spite of this, the Hygroma in her neck continued to grow at an alarming rate. It was decided that Lillian needed Hygroma Surgery now, rather than waiting until she was the proper weight.

Lillian was six months and weighed only sixteen pounds.

It took several weeks to coordinate with the doctor's schedule, so all of them could assist in the surgery. As the day came closer, Brad and Nikki's fear of the unknown became worse. Their poor angel had been so strong. How much more could she endure? In fact, how much more as a family could they endure?

Exhaustion.

Worry.

Fear.

The night before the surgery, Brad and Nikki stayed next to Lillian's crib and did not sleep. Instead, they gazed at their baby girl, watching as she struggled with each breath. The growth was overtaking her body.

Brad and Nikki dreaded what the surgeons were going to do.

Make an incision from behind Lillian's ear.
Continue slicing down to the trachea.
Peel the skin back.
Attempt to remove the disease.
Their baby girl would once again have to fight through the overwhelming odds.

♥

Brad and Nikki sat in the waiting room, receiving updates every half hour by the doctor. Brad was besieged with negative thoughts.

Today is yet another battle to save my daughter.

How many more battles does Lillian have left?

Why couldn't he get along with Nikki anymore? They were once inseparable.

The world is ganging up on me.

Brad gazed at the wedding ring on his finger. It was supposed to be a symbol of his love for Nikki. The ring also represented their eternal faith and devotion to each other. They vowed to spend every day together. "Don't break the streak," they once promised.

Brad lifted his eyes, now looking at Nikki. He realized that they were not fighting together anymore, but rather fighting against each other. Brad slipped off the ring and dropped it in Nikki's purse.

♥

Another update was given by a surgical assistant, followed by another. Hours ticked away, while their little girl laid on the operating table, eyes closed, alone with God.

In all, the surgery took approximately ten hours. 90% of the Hygroma had been removed. A tube was secured in Lillian's face to drain the fluids. After a few hours, the tube had been removed, because it was not working correctly, then replaced back in her tissue.

A few days later, Lillian became stable enough to return home. She had once again beaten the odds.

♥

## A Spiritual Message from Lillian Bay.

*If you become angry with someone, then you must find a way to make peace. Remember it takes at least two people to have an argument. If you develop a gentle spirit, your anger will not grow, but rather your spirit will grow.*

*How much faith, love, and joy are lost when anger becomes our strongest emotion?*

## Lillian Bay, Medical Report

Date: May 21st, 2010

Notes:

- Persistent extensive solid and cystic lesion identified in the neck, consistent with lymphangioma.
- Protrusive vomiting.
- Tongue is somewhat a bluish color.
- Cystic appears a little less prominent.

Lillian Bay Beatty

# Giving Your Heart Away

*"Everyone must be quick to listen, but slow to speak."*

**~ James 1:19**

It was a hot Florida summer evening. Surrounding Brad were thousands of people, many of which were Boca Grande residents. They were quiet, while staring at him. Brad dressed casual in a fishing shirt, shorts, and sandals.

His skin moist with sweat. It was difficult to concentrate. His heart thundered against his chest. More sweat drizzled down his face. The eyes of everyone were on him. He had to be perfect.

Brad stepped on the dirt mound, moving the ball around in his fingers. He was honored to be throwing out the first pitch for the Stone Crabs Baseball team.

Throw it perfectly, he thought.

Do this for both teams.

Do it for the crowd.

Do it for all the people of Boca Grande that are in the stands looking at him.

And most of all, throw it perfectly, so Lillian can watch the crowd applaud for her.

Brad gripped the ball and eyed the catcher. The plate seemed so far away. He lifted his knee, tucked his arm back, and slung the ball with all the force he could throw. The ball snapped into the catcher's mitt with a perfect strike.

The crowd erupted in a massive cheer.

♥

A friend of Brad's wrote out a check and handed it to him. "Take Nikki and Lillian to Washington D.C., on July 4th. You can watch the fireworks from a private area on the wall of the Capitol Building. Everything has been arranged."

This was a chance for Brad and Nikki to revive their marriage. It was a chance for Lillian to do something special.

It was their chance to be a family again.

Lillian was eight months at the time. Brad had to send all her medical supplies in advance. There was an enormous risk in taking Lillian on a plane, but Brad and Nikki refused to deny Lillian of any privilege. The family was going on a vacation, which meant, all three of them were going, no matter what problems the world attempted to throw their way.

At the time, Brad could not have predicted that this would be the first and last time they would take a vacation together.

♥

Brad saw Nikki becoming more distant each day they had been separated, to the point where he could not do anything to draw her back to him. Nikki had shown an endless amount of love and strength.

As a friend.
A daughter.
A sister.
A wife.
A mother.

Nikki agreed to write down her feelings. She used the plane trip as an opportunity to reflect on her life.

❤

**A Spiritual Message from Lillian Bay.**

*The Bible says that love is patient, kind, never jealous, never proud, never selfish, and never rude. I also believe that love can create something new and wonderful. Speaking of new and wonderful, look at me!*

# ISOLATION

*"The righteous should choose his friends carefully, for the way of the wicked leads them astray."*

**~ Proverbs 12:26**

While Nikki became more and more isolated, Brad's difficulties seemed to amplify. He was doing everything he could to help Lillian, while working twelve-hour days and paying the escalating medical bills. Brad also had an idea to start his own business to earn extra money. He asked Nikki if she would support him.

Nikki was vulnerable and looking for her own resolution. Her marriage was falling apart, because of the sizable pressures that never seemed to end. Her and Brad could barely discuss their substantial troubles. Where would they even start?

She was looking for any kind support, just so long as it was not part of her dark world.

Brad's thoughts ran away from him.

Nikki's not thinking clearly.

She's a good person, put in a bad situation.

Brad still loved Nikki. He just wanted his family together again. What could he do?

Make her stay.

Start over.

Stick together.

Never give up.

But it wasn't his choice.

Nikki packed all the necessities, including medical equipment for Lillian, and went to her mother's.

♥

## A Spiritual Message from Lillian Bay.

*The world will continue to move. Days, weeks, months, and years will pass. All God wants for us is to stay pure, even when the world is against us.*

# I Forgive You

*"With the Lord on my side, I do not fear."*

**~ Psalm 118:6**

Nikki promised Brad that she would come back home in a week, but he could not wait that long. Brad drove there with questions swirling in his head.

Is Lillian safe?

Is all the medical equipment setup properly?

Can I convince Nikki to come back home?

Brad parked the car down the street, then walked to the lot next door to where Nikki was staying.

Should I knock on the door?

Can I see my baby?

Should I just leave?

It was late, but he heard voices echoing through the night air. He recognized Nikki and her mother. A few neighbors had joined them on the back porch. They were so loud, Brad could hear every word.

Miserable and dejected, he left.

Shortly after, Nikki moved the rest of her things out of the house.

♥

At that point, Brad knew that his marriage was over. He did not want to accept that reality, but there wasn't much else he could do. Considering what Nikki had gone through with both her father and daughter, she once again searched for a way to start over.

*I had a chance to experience the best of Nikki,* Brad thought.

Brad gave Nikki the divorce she wanted, along with her freedom.

He continued to pray for Nikki and wished only the best for her. Someday she will meet the right person, at the right moment, under the right circumstances. She will find someone that will heal her soul and allow her to look at only the beauty in a world that never stops testing our resilience.

And no matter what, Nikki will continue to be special in Brad's life, because she will always be the mother of Lillian Bay.

♥

## Donations into the Lillian Bay Medical Fund

$100 on June 8th, 2010

$508 on July 9th, 2010

Twenty-two more donations were deposited from residents and businesses of Boca Grande

## A Spiritual Message from Lillian Bay.

*"I forgive you." Sometimes, those three words can be difficult to say. It feels like some people deserve to hear those words, but others do not deserve our forgiveness.*

*The Bible teaches that God has forgiven me for every wrong thing that I have done. That means, God wants me to forgive others, for every wrong thing that they have done.*

*Someday when I am older, I will read this book and learn about all the good and bad that happened in my first years on earth. I can imagine saying words like, "Thank you God for all those people that helped me and thank God for my mother and father."*

*But also, I'll be saying these three words. "I forgive you."*

*Dear Friends*

*"Stop your crying and wipe away your tears. All that you have done for your children will not go unrewarded."*

**~ Jeremiah 31:16**

## Lillian Bay, Medical Report

Date: October 19th, 2010

Notes:

- Enlarged tongue protruding through parted lips, cheeks, chin, and tissue covering jaw, along with enlarged secondary swelling.
- Notable significant facial swelling, including tongue since last surgery.
- Physicians anticipate reduction in swelling as time progresses.
- Lillian is alert, calm, and interactive. Skin tone is a mixture of pale and pink.
- Expressive language skills delayed. Lillian is now using her own translation of signing with hands and fingers gestures, along with communicating via trachea air leak. Most common signs Lillian is using: "Mom, dad, please, and thank you."
- Patient is reacting to the sound of music and even dancing.

Lillian Bay Beatty

♥

*A letter written by Brad, with the help of Archie and Rusty Hager, to the community of Boca Grande.*

Dear Friends,

Most babies are blessed with the ability to grow and develop appropriately and reach their milestones in front of their parents smiling faces. The same goes for my daughter, Lillian Bay. However, for Lillian, it has been a much more difficult, painful, and dangerous road.

Lillian was diagnosed with Cystic Hygroma, which is a series of fluid-filled cysts that have affected her neck, jaw, and mouth, requiring constant medical care. She underwent a surgery to reduce the Hygroma. The swelling after the surgery made it difficult to determine if any new growth of the disease had developed.

Lillian celebrated her first birthday this month, something that seemed like an impossibility considering what she has gone through. While not all the trials and stress are over, I want to make sure Lillian has a good life in any way possible.

Weekly visits to All Children's Hospital in St. Petersburg, Florida are still required, as well as twenty-four hour home nursing care. Lillian is going through speech therapy to help with her difficulties in that area. She is making positive advances each day, but it is still going to be a long journey.

Past donations and fundraisers have helped greatly in staying current with co-pays and medical care, however, your support is still very much needed. Any gifts that can be given would greatly be appreciated.

Trips to the hospital, daily nursing care and medical expenses, along with the daily stress on our family continues to increase. I hope someday I am able to give Lillian a stress free environment to continue growing, along with a Christmas that she absolutely deserves.

With all my heart, I appreciate your prayers and support that have been given by everyone on Boca Grande. Your generous provisions have given Lillian a chance to reach many difficult milestones and accomplish great things in this past year.

Lillian Bay is discovering wonderful and exciting moments in life, just as all children should do.

♥

The letters from insurance companies piled up. To get a better understanding, imagine stacking papers on top of each other, one at a time, until the pile reached two feet.

Brad's private UPS insurance had amazingly covered four million in expenses. However, the bills far exceeded that number. Past donations took out a chunk of the expenses, but the bills continued to pour in, along with threatening letters and phone calls.

Lillian faced a new kind of danger in addition to her disease. She was about to lose her home nursing care, medical equipment, and doctor appointments. Even with all those things, Lillian would still have to fight for her life. But a day without her medical supplies and equipment would end that fight.

Challenged with impending doom, Brad started making phone calls and worked with Sabrina Gilly of the Teamsters Local 79. Meanwhile, he was so appreciative of UPS and all that they had done for him that he did not want his route to suffer on Boca Grande. Brad would use his own time to call high-ranking personnel at all the medical facilities in attempt to work out these problems.

A common exchange between Brad and those making the decisions on Lillian's medical care sounded something like this, "We've been reviewing her medical reports and it seems Lillian is improving, which means, she does not need the extensive medical coverage anymore, especially home nursing."

"Lillian still needs the medical care," Brad pleaded. "The disease has not gone away. She could stop breathing in the middle of the night, or the Hygroma could become worse. Her medical needs cannot be disrupted, especially the home nursing."

"I'm sorry, Mr. Beatty, but we simply do not see it that way. May I suggest you bring your past accounts up to current and then we can speak more on this."

He would not give up. He wrote letters, continued to make phone calls, and relentlessly fought to continue with all of Lillian's medical care, not just a portion. Brad would lose a case, then appeal. He would lose another case, then appeal.

Brad told one high-ranking medical professional, "I will fly with Lillian and stand on your doorstep until you change your mind."

Finally, Brad won his appeal. A decision was made to continue with home nursing and resume all medical treatments without interruption.

## Lillian Bay, Medical Report

Date: February 7th, 2011

Notes:

- The larger cystic components are diminished, however, the extent of infiltrative changes include superficial fascia of the face as well as deeper facial planes.

Lillian Bay Beatty

Multiple surgeries had been done on Lillian, with more surgeries to come. The tumors were not growing, which was extremely good news. However, Lillian was far from being cured of the disease.

Between UPS health insurance and assistance from the Boca Grande community, Brad was able to raise significant money to pay down the medical debt. The insurance also covered sixteen hours of home nursing care and 80% of the medical equipment needed.

Sandy Melvin, owner of Gasparilla Outfitters & Fishing Guide on Boca Grande continued his support. He decided to have a fishing tournament to use as a fundraiser, which raised $4,500.

Once again, the residents of Boca Grande successfully responded to Lillian's needs.

## A Spiritual Message from Lillian Bay.

*It is one thing to stand up for what you believe in. It is entirely different when your life is based on your thoughts. You may not always believe in yourself, but God believes in you.*

*Take some time to think about why you believe in certain things. Why will everything be okay? Why will your troubles not last forever? Why will you live in God's blanket of love?*

*If you understand why you believe, then you will also understand how you will live.*

## Lillian Bay, Medical Report

Date: March 14th, 2011

Notes:

- Incomplete lung expansion with worsened diffuse lung aeration.
- Life support lines are in place.

Lillian Bay Beatty

## Lillian Bay, Medical Report

Date: March 17th, 2011

Notes:

- Moderate to large amount of bilateral abnormal lung opacities. This likely relates to chronic lung disease.
- Pneumonia and worsening respiratory after restarting feeds.
- G-tube and trach dependent based on respiratory difficulty.
- A moderate diffuse airspace disease process continues.

Lillian Bay Beatty

## Lillian Bay, Medical Report

Date: March 23rd, 2011

Notes:

- Moderate diffuse alveolar disease. Most likely include pulmonary edema, pneumonia, and hemorrhage.
- Life support lines are in place.

Lillian Bay Beatty

## Lillian Bay, Medical Report

Date: May 23rd, 2011

Notes:

- Severe fever. Recurring pneumonia.

Lillian Bay Beatty

## Lillian Bay, Medical Report

Date: October 10th, 2011

List of Medications/Treatments:

- Mometasone. Apply to affected area(s) lotion once a day.
- Albuterol. Inhalation nebulizer solution, 1 vial, as needed.
- Mometasone nasal spray. Use in both nostrils once a day.
- Triamcinolone Acetonide. Apply to affected area(s) 2 times daily at the G tube site for 4 weeks, daily for a week and stop.
- Lansoprazole (PREVACID SOLUTAB). Take 1 tablet by mouth every morning. Take 1/2 - 1 hour before food.
- Pediatric Multiple Vit-Vit C. Place 1 mL in gastrostomy tube once a day.
- Acetaminophen drops. Dosage, every 4 hours.
- Dextrose, CONTINUOUS.

Lillian Bay Beatty

## Lillian Bay, Medical Report

Date: October 10th, 2011

List of Medications/Treatments:

- Morphine inj. Every 3 hours.
- OxyCODONE soln. Every 4 hours.
- Ranitidine inj. Every 8 hours.
- Lidocaine buffered inj. Dose once in radiology.
- Doxycycline (IR USE ONLY) Once in radiology.
- Sodium tetradecyl. Once in radiology.

Lillian Bay Beatty

♥

## Donations into the Lillian Bay Medical Fund

$500, on May 26th, 2011

Many more donations were deposited from residents and businesses of Boca Grande

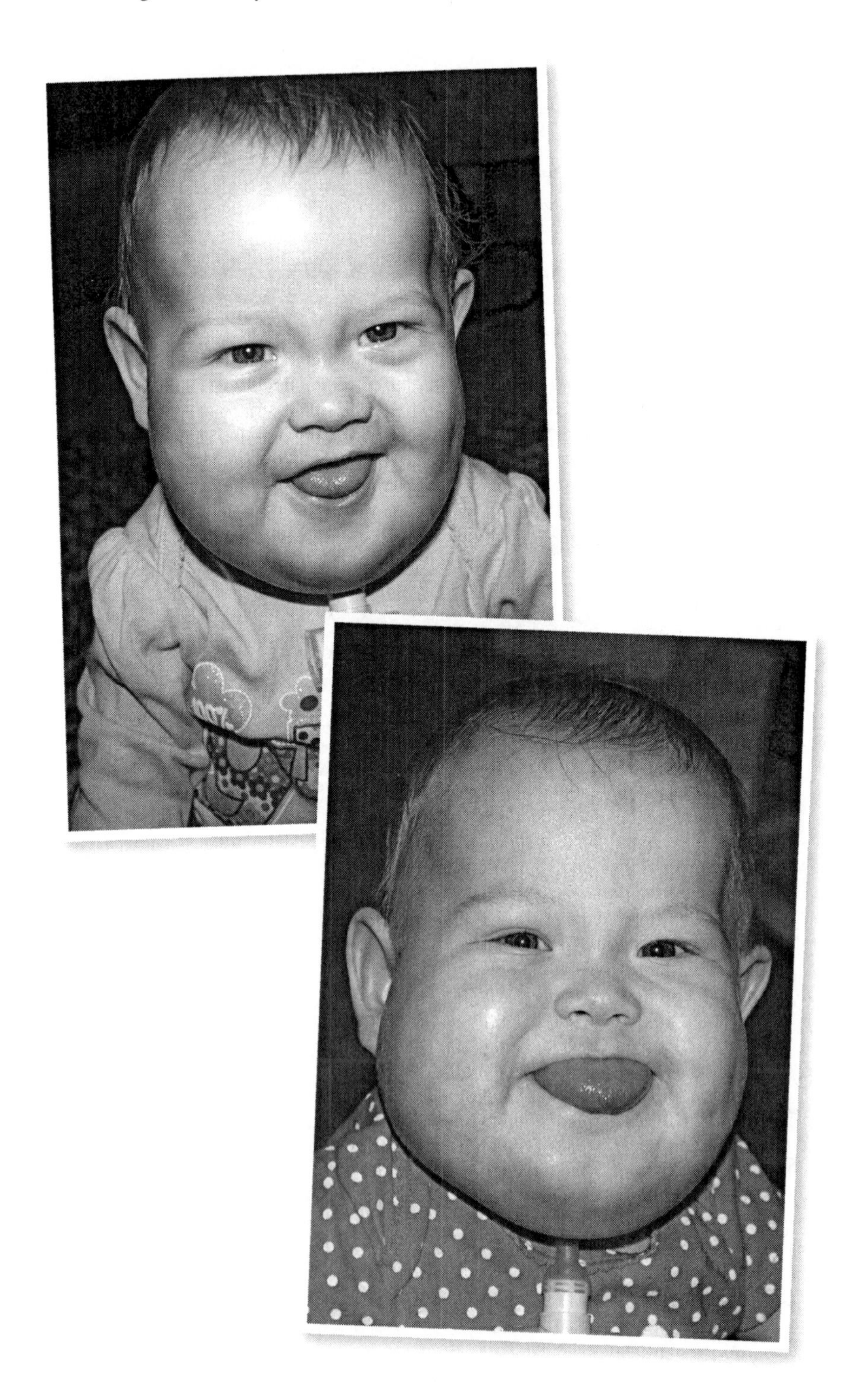

# Angel Getting Her Wings

*"I will heal this city and its people and restore them to health. I will show them abundant peace and security."*

**~ Jeremiah 33:6**

Scar tissue from past surgeries was supposed to soften and eventually go away. Unfortunately, that did not happen. It was decided that another surgery would be needed. It was unknown whether the Hygroma in her throat was completely removed from previous surgeries. Also, doctors were not sure if the Hygroma would spread and become worse.

Once again, the odds were against Lillian.

Dick and Boots (Meredith) Tolsdorf, residents on Boca Grande, took a special shine to Brad and Lillian, spending as much time as possible with them. Boots had connections to the Children's Hospital of Philadelphia. Boots made several phone calls and sent emails stating, "A good friend of mine, Brad Beatty, is desperate to find a way to help his daughter, Lillian. Is there anything you can do?"

A doctor at Children's Hospital of Philadelphia called Brad personally. "Let's make the arrangements to get your daughter to our facility and see if we can help."

♥

Nikki was hesitant about taking Lillian to Philadelphia for a second opinion. Even so, Brad used the next four months to make arrangements with doctors, along with travel plans and hotel accommodations, while continuing to work long hours at UPS and take care of Lillian. Thank goodness, Boca Grande Travel helped with this process to ease the pressure Brad was feeling. One-way tickets were purchased, since the outcome of Lillian's care could not be predicted.

Meanwhile, medical records needed to be sent to Children's Hospital of Philadelphia for their review, which cost a thousand dollars to print and ship.

One of the phone calls Brad made was to Jennifer, who was in charge of patient scheduling. She spent many hours arranging nine appointments for Lillian, along with a possible surgery, depending on the outcome of those appointments. Jennifer explained to Brad, "This kind of thing simply does not happen. You are extremely fortunate to be friends with Boots, or we would not have done all this work."

♥

Dick and Boots Tolsdorf picked Brad and Lillian up from the airport in Philadelphia. Brad had reservations at a home facility that allowed families to stay for free. However, when they arrived, the conditions were unacceptable, so Dick and Boots drove to their house and informed Brad that he and Lillian could stay there.

It was prearranged that all the medical equipment be shipped to the home facility. Brad had to borrow Dick and Boots vehicle and pick up the equipment, then bring it back to their house and set everything up.

Brad was exhausted, as waves of emotions seemed to endlessly crash over him. All these plans, all the favors that were given, and all the time and money spent on an act of faith that this trip would save Lillian's life.

Faith that the doctors appointments would lead to a surgical solution.

Faith that the surgery would work and Lillian would not have to suffer anymore.

Faith that Lillian could have her trach removed and breathe like a normal child.

Faith that Lillian would grow up, continuing to smile and bring joy to others.

♥

Nikki and her mother arrived in Philadelphia and stayed at a Bed & Breakfast in town. With everyone there and the appointments still a day away, Dick and Boots made sure to keep everyone stress free. A good start was to eat a real Philly cheese steak and a tour of Philadelphia, which of course included the Liberty Bell.

Just like the American flag, the Liberty Bell is a symbol of freedom and unity. After the Civil War, the Liberty Bell was taken too many cities in order to heal the country and bring everyone together. Children would say, "When the bell rings, an angel gets its wings."

Brad, Nikki, and Lillian were together in this moment as a family, still searching for a remedy for Lillian's problems.

Unity.

Healing.

Bringing everyone together.

An angel getting her wings.

♥

## A Spiritual Message from Lillian Bay.

*Liberty can mean something different for all of us. It could mean freedom from captivity, burden, or disease. It could be the freedom to make a choice, or to seek wisdom.*

*For me, liberty is the freedom to be a child. No condition, situation, or boundary can limit the joy of who I am.*

*"Proclaim liberty throughout all the land unto all the inhabitants thereof."*

**~ Leviticus 25:10/Inscription on the Liberty Bell**

# Hope Lives Here

*"I assure you, even if you had faith as small as a mustard seed, you could say to this mountain, 'Move from here to there,' and it would move. Nothing would be impossible."*

**~ Matthew 17:20**

The team of doctors at the Children's Hospital of Philadelphia had experience working with children that had a similar condition to Lillian's. Multiple appointments were scheduled and Lillian was ready to take on this challenge.

Friday, October 7th, 2011, 10:30 AM: Plastic Surgery-Vascular Malformation Clinic.

Friday, October 7th, 2011, 12:40 PM: Gastroenterology, Hepatology, & Nutrition.

Thursday, October 13th, 2011, 8:40 AM: Ear, Nose, & Throat.

Thursday, October 13th, 2011, 1:30 PM: Pulmonary.

Friday, October 14th, 2011: Tentatively scheduled for surgery with Dr. Jacobs.

Being considered was a procedure called Sclerotherapy that treats blood vessel malformations. A medicine is injected into the vessels, which makes them shrink, often used in conjunction with laser ablation. In that case, Lillian will have to remain in the hospital for two weeks while excess fluids are being drained.

If successful, there is a chance that the trachea can be removed from Lillian's throat, which has caused many problems such as being constantly blocked and constricting her breathing. Of course, Brad and Nikki considered the procedure for Lillian, but they still had concerns with the mass in her neck and whether or not the disease would eventually grow and spread.

When all the evaluations had been completed, Dr. Jacobs met with Brad and Nikki. "In Lillian's original medical records that were sent from Florida, it was explained that she was a number four-type patient, which means, she has the lowest success rate of being medically treated. However, after doing our own evaluations, we discovered that Lillian is actually a type-one patient."

Brad and Nikki glanced at each other, unable to compute what the doctor was saying. After years of hearing negative news about Lillian, it was difficult to understand that they were actually receiving good news.

Doctor Jacobs looked up from his notes, smiled at Brad and Nikki, then said, "You know what…we can help her."

♥

Surgery was scheduled for Lillian. When they arrived at Children's Hospital of Philadelphia, they waited in the biggest toy room they had ever seen. A little while later, Lillian was admitted into a hospital room and given what's called, "Giggle Juice." Lillian formed the cutest smirk. Her eyes watered, head bobbed up and down, and she laughed as if everything in the room was funny.

Nikki held Lillian, also laughing, while Brad took video on his phone. It was good to see them both smiling, distracted from the thought that Lillian was about to have the most important surgery of her life.

Smiling.

Giggling.

Laughing.

In that room, Brad, Nikki, and Lillian were not afraid. Instead, they decided that this would be a perfect moment of happiness.

"Hope lives here." ~ Children's Hospital of Philadelphia

♥

It was an hour later after the surgery had started when a short female doctor with Irish red hair came inside the waiting room and spoke to Brad. "It looks like All Children's Hospital in St. Petersburg removed most of the Hygroma." She smiled at Brad. "No Sclerotherapy will be performed at this time; perhaps at a later date. Dr. Jacobs is going do some cleaning up, but there's nothing serious to worry about."

When the surgery was complete, Dr. Jacobs met with Brad and Nikki in the hospital room. He told them, "Lillian still has some Hygroma; we cannot be sure if it will start growing again, but for now, this is the best Lillian has been since she was born. In about two months, Lillian will be able to have her trachea removed by All Children's Hospital in Florida."

The next words were not based on low odds of survival, or the chances that Lillian would recover. His words did not paint a grim picture of Lillian's future. Instead, Dr. Jacobs told Brad and Nikki what they had been waiting to hear for the last twenty-three months.

"Lillian is going to be just fine."

♥

Brad did not sleep for the next forty-eight hours. He did not want to rest while Lillian was in recovery. Also, he had to make travel arrangements for them to fly back to Florida, along with shipping all the medical equipment.

On the plane, Lillian sat on one side, Nikki on the other. Both drifted to sleep, resting their heads on Brad's lap. He gently rubbed their backs, still refusing to sleep. For two more hours, they would be a family again. Eventually, the plane would land in Florida. Brad and Nikki would go their separate ways, while taking turns raising Lillian.

The hum of the plane soothed Brad's soul. Clouds were below him with all of the world's problems, while the warm sun comforted and protected them.

Brad thanked God for saving his daughter. He also thanked God for his family, friends, UPS co-workers, the many doctors, nurses, staff, the residents and businesses on Boca Grande, along with all the people that donated their time, treasure, and talent.

Most of all, Brad thanked God for this moment . . . and these blessed two hours with Nikki and Lillian.

♥

## Lillian Bay, Medical Report

Date: November 11th, 2011

Notes:

- Lillian Bay is now two-years-old.
- She is going to be just fine.

Lillian Bay Beatty

♥

## A Spiritual Message from Lillian Bay.

*Peace of mind, body, and spirit can seem so far away.*
*But God's peace is given to us freely.*

*All we need to do is ask.*

# A New Chapter

*". . . I have overcome the world."*

**~ John 16:33**

To put things into perspective, here are just some of the emotions that Brad, Nikki, and Lillian had over the last two and a half years.

Patience.
Hope.
Encouraged by friends.
Dealing with anger.
Listening to your conscience.
Overcoming temptation.
Humility.
Praise.
Anxiety.
Searching for peace.
Loving difficult people.
Timing.
Provision.
Pride.
Assistance.
The desire for answers.
Grace.
Trust.
Staying reliable at work.
Doubt.
Quarrelsome.

Faith.
Confidence.
Reaching out to others.
Kindness.
Spiritual maturity.
Money issues.
Starting over.
Gaining knowledge.
Reputation.
Solitude.
Fighting fear.
Honesty.
Standing up for beliefs.
Understanding God.
Love.
Unselfishness.
Discovering a role in life.
Self-esteem.
Romantic love.
Freedom.
Handling Pain.
Reaching goals.
Finding strength.
Building close relationships.
Sharing faith.
Giving to God.
Spiritual assurance.
Sharing joy.
Rest.
Wisdom.

Was all this a blessing, or a dark part in their lives? Maybe it was both. Nevertheless, I do not believe that Brad, Nikki, and Lillian would trade that time away for anything.

♥

When Brad and Nikki held their baby on her first Christmas night, they understood the probability of not spending a second or third Christmas with their child. In the neighboring rooms of the hospital, two other children had passed away. It was almost impossible not to believe that their child would suffer the same fate.

Perhaps it would be greedy to pray for the safety of their own child, when others near them have died. And if God wants the children to become angels in heaven, then who are we to argue that blessing?

However, children are also needed to be angels on earth.

Lillian's life had been saved. Millions of dollars were needed to help her. Thousands of people used every resource to make this happen. Lillian Bay is alive, because prayers had been answered. But what does the future have waiting for Lillian Bay? How will her life benefit others?

To answer that question, perhaps we should look back on what had been accomplished through Lillian Bay from the time of her birth. Lillian brought together a community of faith, love and prayer. Lillian defied medical odds. She fought through each breath, yet found a way to smile. She fought off the life support machines and found a way to be in peace. She fought through pain, yet found a way to enjoy her life.

If we look back at what had been done through Lillian Bay, then we can look forward, understanding what will happen through Lillian Bay.

People will gather and say, "Show me this miracle. I want to see how a community pulls their resources together with unselfish love to save a child's life. Show me the miracle of a father that refuses to let his daughter be taken from this world. Show me the miracle of a mother that remained strong for her baby during a life threatening birth. Show me the miracle of a child that does not comprehend strength, love, or faith, and yet, displays those gifts with each breath."

People will read her story with tears of hope.

Show me the miracle of Boca Grande. They are an example of a community that believes in giving, more than receiving.

Show me the miracle of a mother that refused to give up on her daughter's life.

Show me the miracle of a father that made decisions based on faith and wisdom.

Show me the miracle of Lillian Bay. She is an example of strength, blessing, and love.

Today, and everyday, let us humble ourselves . . . and be like this child.

Amen.

♥

## A Spiritual Message from Lillian Bay.

*I'm not sure what God has planned for me in the future,*
*or how He will bless my life, or bless the lives around me.*
*But I do know something for sure.*

*This spiritual journey is far from over.*

*"She is strong and respected . . . and not*
*afraid of the future."*

**~ Proverbs 31:25**

# Letters & Stories

## from those Lillian Bay has touched

# Thank You

*"The Lord protects and defends me; I trust in Him. He gives me help and makes me glad; I praise Him with joyful songs!"*

**~ Psalm 28:7**

***Rusty Hager, Chairman of the Board at Hager Company, speaking to the community of Boca Grande.***

Lillian Bay was born with a Cystic Hygroma in her throat and additional Hygroma on her tongue. These types of tumors are benign, but very fast growing. She is a rare survivor with multiple surgeries behind her and additional surgeries to come. The very good news is that the tumors are not getting any bigger, which is a major victory.

To date, the medical bills for Brad have reached into the millions. Joyce Anderson has set up an account at Wachovia Bank on Boca Grande. Joyce will immediately direct the monies donated to reduce Lillian's medical debt. Obviously, this will be a huge burden taken off Brad and Lillian.

Normally I am not involved with situations like this. However, when I first saw Lillian Bay and discovered what this poor child was going through, I could not just stand by and do nothing. Brad is an exceptional person who has navigated through tough decisions and appreciates all the friendship Boca Grande has to offer.

That friendship is what has kept Brad sane…and Lillian Bay alive.

♥

***Letter from Jane, a pediatric nurse for forty years, and a PSA Home Nurse for Lillian Bay.***

Lillian is as an extraordinary child that demonstrates an uncanny awareness of her own needs and those of others, while conveying emotions beyond what is expected of a child at that age. Her social skills are exceptional and endearing to those that meet her.

Lillian Bay has secured a place in my heart.

♥

***Letter from Erin Kostrzewski, a PSA Home Nurse for Lillian Bay.***

Miss Lillian inspires me as a pediatric nurse, because of her strength, courage, and enjoyment of life. Going through major health struggles such as facial surgeries, G.I. problems, and respiratory illness can only combat vast uncertainties for her young life and her family.

With enormous grace and hope achieved by Lillian, she has shown me that love for life can be very contagious. Thus, it gave me a hopeful outlook and the capability to provide extra loving care towards my other patients.

Keeping this in mind, I try to remember how wonderful being happy and healthy can be, no matter what happens in life. I am so pleased to have had the opportunity to spend time caring for Lillian as her nurse. Meeting her and her family has been an uplifting gift.

I wish Lillian a successful future.

♥

**A Spiritual Message from Lillian Bay.**

*Write a thank you letter to a friend. Send a friends card to show that you are thinking of them. Draw a picture for your friend. Help your friend with a tough choice they have to make. Listen to your friend. Pray for your friend.*

*Most of all, think about why you became friends.*

*"A friend loves at all times."*

**~ Proverbs 17:17**

# Creating More Angels

*"We should give special attention to those who are in the family of believers."*

**~ Galatians 6:10**

When people look past the wrongs of the world and discover the beauty, a sense of peace takes over. That is what happened to Amanda York, along with her mother, Ann Marie Nastars, when they strolled into a Target one evening. They weren't really looking for anything, or had a specific reason to be in the store. They just wanted to forget their stressful day.

While walking down the main aisle, a little girl smiled at them. She then waved and said, "Hello." The little girl could not have been much more than two-years-old.

Wanting to keep the women's attention, the little girl made a hugging gesture. The girl's father said, "She's doing her version of sign language." He shook hands with the women and said, "I'm Brad. This is my daughter, Lillian Bay. She's just learning to speak."

Amanda was both intrigued and amazed at the joyful demeanor of Lillian. "What else does she like to do?" Amanda asked.

Brad held his cell phone up. "For some reason, she likes to play the Angry Birds game on my phone."

Through hand gestures, short words, and smiles, Lillian was able to share her love with Amanda and her mother. This resulted in a new reason why they came inside this Target store. They were now on a mission to find an Angry Birds pillow for Lillian!

They hurried up and down the aisles, found a pillow and purchased it. Then, they rushed back to Brad and Lillian. Ann Marie had the pillow in her hand. Lillian's face lit up, as she ran toward Ann Marie and hugged her new gift.

Amanda and Ann Marie had originally gone into Target to walk around and forget about their stressful day. Moments after they entered the store, a two-year-old girl gave them a hug from a distance. With expressions, more than words, Lillian was able to say things like, "Don't sweat the small stuff, ladies." And, "No matter how bad your day is, it's never too late to start your day over with smile."

From this point on, Lillian Bay will be in the hearts of Amanda and Ann Marie. She will encourage others to triumph over the difficulties of the world.

Lillian Bay has taught us to be living angels. We do not need a podium to preach, or millions of dollars to give, or the resources to reach others. Things do not need to be perfect in our lives to spread the gifts of love and hope.

It does not matter how old you are, you can always bring hope and joy to others.

♥

## A Spiritual Message from Lillian Bay.

*To make someone happy, all you need to do is smile and open your arms for a big hug. Bringing joy and love to others means that you cannot focus on yourself. When you are kind to someone, they will learn to be kind to someone else. What a great way to create angels in us all!*

# Cherish Your Family & Friends

*"A friend loves at all times,*
*and a brother is born for adversity."*

**~ Proverbs 17:17**

Ralph Waldo Emerson once said, "God evidently does not intend us all to be rich, or powerful, or great, but He does intend us all to be friends."

As a friend, how do you respond to someone that is going through an extremely difficult situation? What are the correct things to say? In what ways can you be helpful?

Sue is part of the Boca Grande community. Like so many others on Boca Grande, she became friends with Brad. She saw how excited Brad was when he first announced that he was going to be a father. Sue witnessed Brad keeping his faith when he was informed that the baby was going to have many difficulties.

As a parent of two children, Sue also knows that your children come first, and that every moment spent with your children is precious. When Lillian Bay was born, Sue could not understand how a baby could suffer so much, from the moment she entered the world.

Sue witnessed the energy being taken away from Brad. She

could see the agony wipe away his high spirits. As a friend, she anxiously waited for updates from Brad, listening to the complexities of Lillian's disease, along with the scenarios of good news and bad news.

The weeks went by and Brad was spending every second possible with Lillian. Sue wondered how many more days Brad would continue working this hard and go without sleep. When would the exhaustion overtake his once faithful spirit? How would Brad keep up with the ever-growing medical bills?

As a friend, what do you say? What are the perfect words to comfort someone that is overwhelmed physically, mentally, financially, and most of all, spiritually? Sue did not want to say something like, "Don't worry, everything will be okay."

In her office on Boca Grande, Sue folded her hands and prayed.

She then witnessed God's love and friendship. Support came from the Boca Grande community, along with surrounding areas on the island. Fundraisers and events were put together to help the family.

God's favor did not stop there. Sue witnessed Brad's renewed energy, as he continued to fight to save Lillian. The community of friends added their prayers and immeasurable support.

As a friend, Sue would like to share these words of wisdom. "People change, things change, and we fight for what we believe in, and we fight even harder for those we love. Sometimes when you think you are all alone, it takes a little reminder that many people love and support you even if you do not see it. I have learned to hug my children a little tighter and truly cherish my family."

Sue also suggests that you take a look around. While at a community event, look at the other people. While at church, look at the others in the pews. While at work, look at the employees and customers.

Remember that each person has a story to tell and it is a blessing if that person becomes your friend . . . and shares their story with you.

♥

Dear Lilly:

When you were born, it was a special day. You came out of Mommy with so many problems that we were unsure of your future. But Daddy and Mommy had so much faith that you were going to grow up and be a wonderful lady. I am your Daddy's mommy. From the very beginning, I was there for you. I helped in so many different ways even though I was a little afraid of handling you and caring for you until you got a little older. I did what I could until the time when you and Daddy were alone and then I was blessed to step in and help Daddy take care of you.

You have been a constant blessing to me to watch you grow, not only in days and months, but also in health. We have had so much fun together. We have giggled, played, read, and of course played on my iPAD. You know how to use it. How to look at all the pictures and how to play the games. You are amazing!

I love you more than life itself. I am so happy to be your Gamma!! I am so looking forward to spending so much time with you as you grow up. We have a special bond between us, which will continue to grow as you become all that God wants you to be.

Gamma

♥

## A Spiritual Message from Lillian Bay.

*God can use my friends to help me grow. In fact, when you show friendship to others, YOU are growing! All the friends around you are a gift from God. You may not know what to say when a friend is hurting. Pray to God and ask Him what to do.*

*When I see all the new friends I have, the best way to show how much I love them is to give them a great BIG SMILE! And don't forget about your closest friend . . . JESUS!*

# Never Forget Those Moments

*"The prayer of a good person has a powerful effect."*

**~ James 5:16**

The Palm on the Park team went to see a bluegrass band on the 3rd Street Beach Access while the sun was setting. Not all of the people there knew each other, but something amazing happened. Lillian was stomping her feet, hopping up and down, laughing and dancing. As the sun dipped behind the island and the music continued, Lillian was able to bring everyone together through smiles and laughter. The 3rd Street crowd became friends and joined with the dancing angel.

That night, Kris Boyden from Palm on the Park thanked God over and over for Lillian Bay. "She is living proof that prayer works."

♥

Lillian Bay has a fourteen-year-old aunt named, Madison Beatty. The first time she saw her niece was eleven days after Lillian was born. Her first reaction was how small Lillian was, yet how big her smile was on her face. "We have the same eyes," Madison said with pride. She stared at the baby, anticipating her future with confidence.

Inside that hospital room, Madison made a decision that Lillian was going to be the most important person in her life. Lillian will flash her smile and make others smile as well.

Every Sunday, Madison made the trip with her mother to visit Lillian. Being fourteen, she had a busy schedule with school and friends, but all she could think about was getting to the hospital every Sunday, no matter what.

Madison witnessed the challenges Lillian had to endure. During some visits, Lillian would be strong, breathing well, and fighting with unimaginable strength. Other visits, Lillian struggled with each breath, or had pneumonia, which prevented Madison from being able to hold her niece.

Madison continued to visit, praying that Lillian would have the strength to keep fighting from Sunday to Sunday.

♥

In January, Lillian was able to go home. Madison could see the beauty in Lillian's smile, along with the never-ending struggles in Lillian's eyes. Madison just wanted her little angel to be okay.

She turned to God and prayed, night after night, "Please help Lillian to get better. Allow Lillian to experience life, just as I have." Madison did not want to be angry with God, nor question His guidance in our lives. Even so, she was honest with her prayers. "Oh God, after everything Lillian has gone through, she deserves to live."

♥

On Halloween, Brad and Madison dressed Lillian up as Tinker Bell, a character that is described as, "A symbol of the magic of Disney." They took Lillian to a festival in downtown Boca Grande, where other children had already been judged for their costumes. However, the Boca Grande judges were kind enough to allow Lillian to enter and they presented her with an extra award. Lillian gave them a magical smile in return.

♥

To correct Lillian's speech, the doctor instructed Brad to carefully place a passy muir (speaking) valve on Lillian. Suddenly, Madison and Brad could hear Lillian making random noises. They sat down in front of Lillian and just listened to her voice. Lillian was giggling and making strange, yet funny sounds.

Madison said, "I'll never forget this moment."

♥

They decorated the Christmas tree with Lillian. Brad handed Lillian the star, then picked her up like an angel, watching as Lillian placed the star at the top of the tree.

Afterwards, Madison made chocolate chip cookies. She gave Lillian one, but did not expect her to eat it. Lillian pushed her finger down on the melted chocolate and placed her gooey fingers in her mouth. Lillian then gave Madison a chocolate smirk. Also,

Lillian pointed to the cookies . . .
The angel wanted more.

♥

In March of 2011, Lillian had taken a turn for the worse. Madison felt helpless as the cheery expression of Lillian weakened and she became more and more sick. Madison had always been able to make Lillian smile, but now, Lillian's eyes became distant and unresponsive, as her health deteriorated.

Madison was heartbroken, wanting so badly to help her precious angel.

Lillian was rushed to the hospital. Madison's mind was plagued with the unknown. All she could think about was that the doctors still did not have enough research to cure Lillian's disease.

Madison and Brad stayed at the hospital overnight. Machines beeped in the hospital room and nurses kept coming and going. Madison needed a few hours of sleep, but if Lillian could not rest, then neither would she.

Every hour or so, Madison would use the sink to splash cold water on her face. She would gaze at Lillian, willing her to keep breathing.

Keep fighting.

You're such a strong little angel.

At four o'clock in the morning, Brad handed Madison a key. "This will open the main door so you can leave and come back. I want you to get out of the room for a while. Walk around the hospital and clear your head."

Madison listened to her big brother and reluctantly took a walk around the hospital. That's when she found a small chapel. She went inside, eased down to her knees, folded her hands, closed her eyes and prayed.

A couple of hours later, Madison went to the lobby and looked out the window. Her eyes were glossed with exhaustion. She fixated on the darkness until the sun began to rise. She gazed at the sunbeams, chasing away the long night, bringing hope to a new day.

Madison turned, seeing a nurse that had just come off the third shift. The nurse forced a tired grin and said, "How are things with you? Are you okay?"

"I'm good," Madison said, returning an exhausted smile.

Madison thought about the nurses and doctors at All Children's Hospital, how they cared deeply for their patients and the families with infinite kindness.

Madison thanked God for the All Children's staff. Lillian was alive because of them.

♥

February of 2012, Madison walked into the house, seeing a little girl's face light up with excitement and then shouting, "Aunt Maddie!" The little girl ran to Madison and gripped her in a hug.

The little girl ran around the house, then took a break to draw a picture. She played with stuffed animals, jumping up and down with an abundance of energy. Her pale skin had been replaced with a dash of Florida color.

Brad and Madison dressed the little girl up in a glittery skirt and took her bowling. The angel had her own scoring system and yelled after each game, "I won!"

First thing on Sunday, the little girl would climb up on the beds and wake her dad, then wake up her aunt. Unlike everyone else in the family, this angel seemed to be a chipper morning person. She refused to start the day with anything but a smile, followed by an animated laugh.

Brad, Madison, and the little angel went to church. Then,

Madison took the little girl for an adventure throughout the church, into the garden, and around the block.

Residents of Boca Grande saw Madison with the little girl. They would smile and say, "My goodness, is that Lillian Bay? She is getting so big!"

Madison squeezed Lillian's hand and whispered to herself, "Yes she is."

## A Spiritual Message from Lillian Bay.

*Family and friends.*

*Sunday mornings.*

*Chocolate chip cookies.*

*Drawing pictures.*

*Stuffed animals.*

*Jumping up and down.*

*Smiling.*

*Hugging.*

*Dressing up for Halloween.*

*Bowling in a glittery outfit.*

*Church.*

*Hanging a star at the top of a Christmas tree.*

*Walking in a garden.*

*Strolling around the block.*

*Saying hello to people on a perfect sunny day.*

*May God bless every moment in your life.*

*"At day's end, I am ready for sound sleep, for you, God, have put my life back together."*

**~ Psalm 4:8**

# Impossible Decision

*"Seek His will in all you do,*
*and He will direct your paths."*

**~ Proverbs 3:6**

Ron and Jill had just been married when they found out that they were going to have a baby. During a sonogram, the doctor informed them that there were complications with the baby. However, the doctor was unfamiliar with the problem and sent Jill to a specialist.

That is when they were informed that the baby had Cystic Hygroma. The head was the shape of lemon, because fluid pressed against the temples. There was also fluid in the baby's lungs and the kidneys were underdeveloped.

The doctor advised Ron and Jill to terminate the pregnancy.

Ron and Jill, Catholics and Pro Life, had to make an impossible decision.

Jill stopped answering the phone. She refused to go out, or take visitors. Instead, she wanted to be alone with her husband and unborn child, away from a world that had stolen their joy . . . and hope.

Both Jill and Ron did not understand why this was happening to them. They went to church, prayed, read the bible, and did everything they could to help others. Why had this burden been placed on them?

Most of all, why were they being forced to decide the fate of their baby?

Ron began doing research on Cystic Hygroma. He discovered that in some rare cases, the baby survives. However, in these cases the parents and doctors claimed that it was simply a miracle, because the chances of survival were about zero.

A decision had to be made by Ron and Jill . . .

♥

Above was an example of husband and wife going through similar circumstances as Brad and Nikki. I do not know what Ron and Jill decided, but I do know that many others have to make an equal tough decision.

"For the past few weeks my life has been an emotional roller coaster. Our unborn baby has Cystic Hygroma on the back of the neck. We demanded a second opinion as I refused intrusive tests that could risk miscarriage. I was also advised termination of the pregnancy, because of the size and severity of the Hygroma condition."

Another example. "The doctor is saying that the baby still has a small chance, but that if we see a decrease in the Hydrops and the Cystic Hygroma that chance becomes much greater. I go for another sonogram in two weeks and I am very anxious. I keep hoping and praying that everything will turn out fine. We found out that we are having a little boy. Please let me know if anyone else has experienced this. Thank you again for your prayers and thoughts. We need all we can get."

Another example. "I just found out that our baby has Cystic Hygroma. We got a second opinion and had another ultrasound. The results were not the same. They are now thinking that the baby has Down Syndrome, because the thickness around the neck is compatible with Downs. So two tests show two different things. I was scheduled to have the pregnancy terminated on January 14th. I can't help but feel that there is nothing wrong with our baby because of what is happening, but I don't want to get my hopes up either. Somebody . . . please give me advice."

♥

Many doctors that diagnosis Cystic Hygroma before birth recommend termination of the pregnancy. Parents are also told that even if the baby survives the birth, the chances are low that the child will continue living. However, there is little research to support this recommendation to parents.

Children born with Cystic Hygroma need specialized clinics, detailed studies, accurate counseling, and financial support for medical costs and out of pocket expenses.

We need to make sure every child with Cystic Hygroma has at least a chance to survive.

Lillian Bay is LIVING proof.

# LITTLE FLOWER

*"These things we write to you . . . that your joy may be full."*

**~ 1 John 1:14**

In 1935, the mayor of New York City, Fiorello LaGuardia, showed up at a night court in the poorest district in the city. He dismissed the judge for the evening and took over the bench. Mayor LaGuardia was a short man, only five feet tall, nicknamed, Little Flower.

That night, a tattered old woman, charged with stealing a loaf of bread from a shopkeeper, was brought before him. The old woman defended herself by saying, "My daughter's husband has deserted her. She is sick, and her children are starving."

The shopkeeper stepped forward and said, "It's a bad neighborhood, your honor. She has to be punished in order to teach other people a lesson."

The mayor sighed, while gathering his thoughts. He gazed at the old woman and said, "I have to punish you. The law makes no exceptions. You must either pay ten dollars, or spend ten days in jail." While pronouncing the sentence, Mayor LaGuardia reached into his pocket, took out a ten-dollar bill, and threw it into his hat. "Here's the ten dollar fine, which I now remit. Furthermore, I'm going to fine everyone in the courtroom for living in a town where a person has to steal bread so her grandchildren can eat." He looked at the Bailiff. "Collect the fines and give them to the defendant."

The shopkeeper, seventy defendants, and a few New York police officers dropped money into the hat.

LaGuardia was said to be one of the greatest mayor's in modern U.S. history. And of course, one of the world's greatest airports was named after him. (Not bad for a guy that was nicknamed, "Little Flower.")

It may seem impossible for an entire country to help its citizens. It may seem impossible for a state, a city, or even a town to rally around its citizens.

Perhaps we need a place to start. I believe that when someone in our community is in need, our first reaction should be to pray and ask for wisdom. "How can I help, Oh Lord? How can I bring the community together? What should I do first?"

When someone in the community has fallen both emotionally and spiritually, we need to gather the residents and help that person rise back up. When you or I fall, God will bring the community together, helping us to rise up once again.

Boca Grande is an example of a community that refused to let a family suffer. Kris Boyden, Manager at Palm on the Park, said it perfectly. "If Brad was in New York City, or any other big city, he would be just some guy with a sad story to tell. We are so thankful he's here on the Boca Grande where we can all help him spiritually and financially!"

Boca Grande is certainly a beautiful community, but it is the inner beauty of the residents and businesses that makes them so special.

# SPIRITUAL PATH

*"God has given me the wonderful privilege of telling everyone about this plan of His; and He has given me His power and special ability to do it well."*

**~ Ephesians 3:7**

My name is Ron Knight, the author of Saving Lillian Bay. You are probably wondering why I waited until now to introduce myself. It's because I'm only a smart part of this story.

Looking back on the path God had sent me on, it was difficult for me to understand what God had planned in my life. I'm telling you this, because there will be humbling moments where you will question God, plead for His mercy, and it will appear that God has distanced Himself from you.

Consider the spiritual circumstances that God put in motion for me years ago:

• From 1986 to 1989, I worked as a contract sorter for McGraw-Hill Publishing. My position was replaced by a computer.

• I was a courier at FedEx from 1989 to 2002, while writing books in my spare time and dreaming of becoming an author.

• On November 7th, 2002, I was in a work related accident that was not my fault, but the extensive injuries ended my career at FedEx. To this day, I am still feeling the pain.

• From 2002 to 2007, I owned a board game business and continued to be a part-time author.

• In 2007, like many businesses, we were forced to shut down. I decided to become a full time author.

• In 2009, I collaborated with a wonderful branding agency that would market and publish my books. The company is called, Brand Eleven Eleven. My wife and I were married on 11-11, so we thought it was fate that I partnered with this terrific business. (Note: On 11-11-09, Lillian Bay was born.)

• By the spring of 2011, I had written over twenty novels, with more in the works. I also released my first middle school book, which was doing extremely well.

• In the fall of 2011, I released a second middle school book and had over one hundred planned speaking engagements. For some unknown reason that I still cannot explain, the book sales were low and the speaking engagements never came to fruition.

• Because of the terrible fall sales, I had to take a seasonal position at UPS to earn some extra money so that I could help pay our bills and purchase a couple of gifts for my wife and four children, and a small gift for Melissa, the owner of Brand Eleven Eleven. I was feeling guilty at the time, because my wife, children, and publisher had supported me in hopes that my career as an author would take off and have significant rewards. It looked more as if my career was coming to an end.

• Over the month of December, my body took a horrific beating at UPS. I wanted to quit several times, but my family needed the money. Every delivery I made, every step to every door, was pure agony.

• After one of my UPS shifts, I arrived home in the evening and could barely walk. I was just about to shower and collapse on the couch when a UPS manager called and said, "We have a driver named Brad who delivers on Boca Grande that is in big trouble. He desperately needs your help. Is there anyway you can come back in to work?" Despite the pain, I agreed to go and help the driver.

• Just before leaving, I noticed my wife and kids staring at me. They wanted me to quit the UPS job. "You weren't meant to work there," my wife said. "You were born to be an author and that's all you should be doing." But for some reason, I had to do this. I wobbled to my car and headed to Boca Grande.

• It took me forty-five minutes before I arrived at the tollbooth on Gasparilla Island, which leads to Boca Grande. Unfortunately, the toll was $5.00 and they would only accept cash, which I did not have on me.

• I drove twenty minutes in the direction I had just come from and withdrew money from an ATM. I had to use the restroom, but the driver on Boca Grande had been waiting for me, so I skipped the bathroom stop and hurried back to the tollbooth.

• A UPS manager had also arrived at the tollbooth. I introduced myself to the manager and explained my delay. The manager had me park my car and ride with him in the truck. The tollbooth operator changed his mind and said there was no need for me to pay the $5.00 fee. (Uggg.)

• It was pitch-black on Boca Grande. I'd never been on the island before and the UPS manager was unfamiliar with the maze of streets. It took another forty-five minutes to locate Brad.

• While I was helping Brad, he opened up to me about his daughter and practically told me the entire story in twenty minutes. I was so moved by that spiritual moment, I blurted out an idea that I could write a book that would be special to Lillian and possibly help with any medical expenses. Brad was overjoyed and agreed without giving it a second thought.

• In January of 2012, I collected all of Brad's notes, pictures, medical reports, insurance reports, past articles, and donation receipts. The pile was big enough to cover my dining room table. I then began reading through everything and wrote the story.

• On March 30th, 2012, my family and I were scheduled to stay with Brad on Boca Grande for the weekend, which would give us a chance to meet Lillian Bay. About two weeks before the mini-vacation, Brad called. "I won't be there on March 30th, Lillian was just scheduled for surgery on that day."

"What kind of surgery?" I asked.

Then, I could almost envision the smile on Brad's face. "Lillian is going to get her trach taken out! She's going to be breathing on her own!"

"That is so awesome," I said. "I am so happy for you and Lillian."

"Lillian and I will still meet you on Boca Grande, but not until the next day. So take your family and have fun until we get there."

• My family and I arrived on Boca Grande on Friday, March 30th, astonished by the beautiful four bedroom/four bath beach home. (Which a business owner on Boca Grande let us stay for free.) Also staying with us was Brad's mother, who we met for the first time.

• On Saturday, March 31st, 2012, my family and I had the privilege of meeting Lillian Bay. My first moment with her was when she walked out of a local grocery store on Boca Grande, carrying a box of chocolate donuts. Lillian handed the donuts to her grandmother, then crawled up on the golf cart. She gave my son, Zach, a big hug. (We later discovered that Lillian and Zach would become like brother and sister.)

I smiled at Lillian and said, "Hey there. My name is Mr. Knight and I'm writing a book about you."

Lillian looked at me, smiled, reached out with both hands, then pulled me close to her with a loving hug.

It was a perfect sunny day, with a vivid blue sky, and a cool sea breeze mixed with warm air. Lillian was wearing a pink dress, with matching pink shoes and sunglasses.

Brad and Lillian were just coming off a two and half year struggle. The last two and half years of my life, and the lives of my wife and four children, had also been a struggle. But that day, all of us knew that the struggles had been worth it.

God had brought us together with the promise of a spiritual

future, filled with love and hope.

♥

Looking back, everything that happened made perfect sense, even if I did not see it at the time. It was a long, tough rode to this point. I could have changed directions and done something else besides being an author, but I kept on the path, believing that God knew exactly what He was doing with my life.

I also believe that whatever books I write in the future, will not be as important as this one.

I'm blessed that God trusted me with His plan. Most of all, I am blessed to have the love and trust of Brad and Lillian Bay, my wife Terry, my son Zachary, my daughter Samantha, my daughter Kayci, and my daughter Kiana, along with my business partner and dearest friend at Brand Eleven Eleven, Melissa.

Thank you God for all that you have done for us.

♥

*I dedicate Saving Lillian Bay to my mother. After her death, she left behind hundreds of books for me to read.*

*Brad Beatty would like to dedicate this book to Nurse Bev Fann, along with all those family and friends who passed away.*

# Sources for Saving Lillian Bay:

Notes/Interview/Photos *
Medical Records, All Children's Hospital *
All Children's Hospital Website
Boca Beacon
Cystic Hygroma Support Group
Community Baby Center, Cystic Hygroma
Wikipedia
John R. Walter
Pediatric Services of America.
Good News Bible, Today's English Version
Checklist for Life, by Thomas Nelson Publishing
Boca Grande Fire Department
Medical Records, Children's Hospital of Philadelphia *
Harpoon Harry's Website
Fox News, Tampa, YouTube
Kris Boyden & Jennifer Burch, Palm on the Park, Boca Grande
Multiple Insurance Letters *
Rusty Hager, CEO & Chairman of the Board, Hager Company
Archie Hager, COO Hager Company
S.M.A.R.T. Monitor Handbook
Multiple Letters Mailed to Boca Grande Residents *
Medical Records, Ian N. Jacobs, Otolaryngology *
Medical Records, Lauren K. Lewis, RN *
Medical Records, Christopher M. Cielo, DO *
Medical Records, Joanne Stow, CRNP *
Medical Records, N Scott Adzick, MD *
Report, Maternal Fetal Medicine in Port Charlotte *
Report, Dr. Gregush, Obstetrician *
Report, Dr. Washington Hill *

Medical Records, Dr. Thomas Andrews, an Ear Nose and Throat Specialist *
Medical Records Dr. Karen A. Raimer *
Report, Gastroenterologist at Hepathology and Nutrician in both Florida and Pennsylvania *
Medical Report Dr. Susan Williams, Pediatrician *
Marsha Dollins
Report, Bayfront Medical Center *
Report, Gasparilla Properties on Boca Grande *
Ronald McDonald House
Crowninshield Community House Spaghetti Dinner Benefit *
Power Thoughts, by Joyce Meyer
Jane, Pediatric Nurse (Last name withheld)
Erin Kostrzewski, PSA Home Nurse
Liberty Bell Facts/History
Report, Plastic Surgery-Vascular Malformation Clinic *
Fundraising Deposit Slips, Englewood Bank, Boca Grande *
Fundraising Deposit Slips, Wells Fargo Bank, Boca Grande *
Joyce Anderson, Wachovia Bank on Boca Grande *
Poor Parental Advice Group
Amanda York
Ann Marie Nastars
Sue Schultz
Madison Beatty
Ron Knight Bio/History
Other photographs provided by Brand Eleven Eleven

* Provided by Brad Beatty

Thank you to all the contributors who participated in our Indiegogo campaign to make this possible. A special thanks to:

Customers of Fugates, Fugates, Igrales, Paul Noller, Cynthia Johnstone, Cynthia Bender, Sherry Butler, John Molle, Lisa Arundale, Robert Polito, Mildred Fugere and several amazing anonymous donors. Without your support this project would not have been possible.

To learn more about Lillian Bay and Cystic Hygroma, please go to www.savinglillianbay.com

For more books by Ron Knight, go to www.authorronknight.com

CPSIA information can be obtained at www.ICGtesting.com
Printed in the USA
LVOW100704071212

310517LV00005B/12/P